Enough Already!

Breaking Free in the Second Half of Life

BRUCE O'HARA

New Star Books | Vancouver | 2004

New Star Books Ltd.

107 – 3477 Commercial Street | Vancouver, BC V5N 4E8 | Canada
1517 Gulf Rd., #1517 | Point Roberts, WA 98281 | USA
info@NewStarBooks.com | www.NewStarBooks.com

Publication of this work is made possible by grants from the Canada Council, the British Columbia Arts Council, and the Department of Canadian Heritage Book Publishing Industry Development Program.

Conseil des Arts du Canada   Canada Council for the Arts   Canada   BRITISH COLUMBIA ARTS COUNCIL

Printed on 100% post-consumer recycled paper. Printed and bound in Canada by Imprimerie Gauvin. First printing, October 2004

LIBRARY AND ARCHIVES CANADA CATALOGUING IN PUBLICATION

O'Hara, Bruce, 1952–
Enough already! : breaking free in the second half of life / Bruce O'Hara.

Includes bibliographical references and index.
ISBN 1-55420-010-5

1. Middle aged persons — Conduct of life. 2. Older people — Conduct of life. 3. Simplicity. 4. Self-actualization (Psychology) I. Title.

BJ1691.033 2004   158.1'084'4
C2004-905187-3

To my daughter, Zoey:

The adventurous and playful spirit with which you embrace your youthful freedom reminds me, as I enter a new, almost-youthful freedom of my own, of the infectious power of enthusiasm.

Acknowledgements

A heartfelt thanks to my Feedback Circle: David Stott, Pam and Don Munroe, Norm Reynolds, Nancy Stern, Lois Faris, Karen and Don Clarke, Bill Massey, Sam Sommers, Tom Walker and Maggi Rayment. You didn't just improve the book; you made it more fun to write. Particular thanks to Tom and Maggi for your thoroughness and your insight.

Thanks to my partner, Adriana, for regularly burying me in helpful resources — all writers should be so fortunate as to have an in-house librarian — and for setting up the reward of those glorious months in Spain as an incentive to actually finish. And, oh yes — thank you for your patient understanding on those many occasions when I was "lost in the book."

I would like to express my appreciation to everyone who shared with me their personal experience of the feelings, joys, and challenges of the second half of life. You made it real to me in a way that no expert could.

I am grateful to my editor, Audrey McClellan, for being both gentle and firm, and for that knack you have of cleaning up my clumsiness without losing my voice. Finally, I want to thank New Star publisher Rolf Maurer for steadfast encouragement and support in nurturing this project to fruition.

Bruce O'Hara

August 2004

Contents

Enough Already!

What Are You Doing
for the Rest of Your Life?

What are you doing for the rest of your life? Shortly after my fiftieth birthday I wrote the following:

> My experience of living as a free being — coping quite comfortably on an income close to Canada's official poverty line — is that life feels so good it's almost scary. I wake up most mornings grateful to be alive. I have to tell you, when I was a wage slave I had some interesting and enjoyable jobs, but I did not generally wake up feeling grateful!
>
> It is luxurious, finally having enough free time in my life. Time to relax, to socialize, to read, to play, to exercise, time to think. Not so much that I feel aimless or bored, but enough to feel time-rich. It's also easier to have an intimate, playful, and sensuous relationship with my partner when we're not tired or stressed out.
>
> In some ways it feels like being twenty again, in that there's a world full of exciting choices. The hardest part is deciding what to do first.

The title "Enough Already" comes from a phrase I keep hearing. Sometimes it's said in frustration, sometimes with petulance, often with impatience, and always with longing — a longing that sometimes doesn't even have a name, but a longing nonetheless.

This book is written for my generation, the baby boomers, all ninety million of us. The oldest of the boomers are well into life's second half. Even the youngest are only a few years shy of entering the second half of life.

So far, only a small minority of boomers have taken up the "Enough Already" cry, but our number is growing, as you will see. That this book is in your hands suggests you may be getting ready to join us.

If at forty-something or fifty-something you feel a yearning to break free of old patterns, your friends may dismiss it as a "mid-life crisis." Conventional wisdom has it that a mid-life crisis is like a delayed attack of adolescence, a yearning after lost youth.

Perhaps. But I believe the impatience that expresses itself as "Enough Already" more likely springs from a recognition of the new choices opening up at mid-life: not a mid-life crisis but a *mid-life opportunity.*

The mid-life opportunity emerges as a result of several important changes that happen for most people sometime during their fourth or fifth decade:

✧ **Parental responsibilities diminish.** At first it's as simple as being able to go out without having to find a babysitter. Then, as your kids leave home, a larger freedom beckons. When your kids pass beyond needing help with schooling costs, a whole new range of choices opens.

✧ **Nesting commands less of your attention.** If you've found the home you want, furnished it to your tastes, and accumulated a goodly supply of tools and toys, the energy that used to go to nesting is free for something new.

✧ **You may be overdue for a career change.** If you've spent twenty or thirty years in one career, you may have learned what you wanted to learn and achieved all you wanted to achieve. And sometimes, ready or not, a rapidly changing economy may turf you out of your comfortable old job.

✧ **New financial leeway may appear.** Once the kids leave home, some old expenses disappear. Perhaps you make the last payment on your house mortgage. Perhaps an older relative dies and leaves an inheritance. Perhaps you downshift to a smaller home in a less expensive neighbourhood. As an experienced older worker, you often have a better income and more choices in the workplace.

✧ **With luck you become older but wiser.** By the time you reach mid-life you may have achieved enough maturity to not care what others think. The dawning recognition that you will get old, and you will die, may spur you to pursue dreams you put on hold when your kids were young.

All these changes mean there are real opportunities to live life differently in the second half of life — not at sixty-five, but at forty-five and fifty-five.

The New Frame of the Second Half

Our standard view of the life cycle is the triad of study/work/ retire. You go to school till you're twenty-something, work full-time till you're sixty-something, then retire.

If this frame has a payoff for those in middle age, it is in the assumed subtext of working = young and retired = old. We push off into the future whatever fears we might have about growing old.

The problem with the study/work/retire life-cycle model is that it makes the period from twenty-five to sixty-five seem all of a piece. It makes it seem like a fifty-year-old has far more in common with a thirty-five-year-old than with a sixty-five-year-old. In truth, our tasks, challenges, and opportunities at age fifty-five are quite different from what they were when we were thirty-five.

At fifty-five, whether you know it or not, you are forming the template for your life at sixty-five and seventy-five. Whether you notice it or not, much of the freedom we usually associate with retirement is already available to us. The idea that you are somewhere in the middle of the same-old same old of working life can cause you to sleepwalk through what could be an exciting new adventure.

My suggestion: Stop viewing your life through the flawed lens of study/work/retire. If you are forty-something or older, think of yourself instead as entering *the second half of your life*. Doing so will open you to experiencing the second half of life as a new adventure with new opportunities.

When I use the phrase "the second half of life," I do not mean it in a sentimental way, the way people often talk of older retirees as being in their "golden years." I'd like to play a bit of "what if?" with you. What if you substantially reduced your work-week at age fifty? What if you then lived like the happiest of North American seniors and, like them, lived hale and hearty twenty years beyond the norm? (I'll talk about how they do it in Chapter Nine.) You could, if you're reasonably lucky, live to be a hundred, spending fully half the days of your life in a new freedom. Even if you only live to eighty-two — the projected average life expectancy of the boomer generation — that's thirty-two years of a new life, as long as or longer than the time you spent in the full-time workforce.

Freedom Now!

This is not a pre-retirement guide. There are already boxcars of books on "how to be happy in retirement." The world doesn't need another. This book is about finding freedom *now,* at the beginning of the second half of life.

Retirement is the bait-and-switch offered to anyone having a mid-life crisis. Your friends tell you, "Be patient. Everything will be puddle-wonderful once you get to the promised land of retirement." What it means is: Deprive yourself of freedom now so that you can be really free later.

How do you feel about retirement? Ambivalent perhaps? Does the idea of retiring make you antsy? Why would that be?

Spend a few minutes personalizing your hopes and fears for retirement. Begin combing your memory for all the old and older people you have known over the years. (Yes, I know, your parents seemed "old" when they were your age, but I mean really old, older than you are now!) See if you can locate examples of the following:

✦ Can you think of someone who was unhappy in retirement? Someone who was bored or lost, who felt useless or was depressed?
✦ Can you think of people who put off retiring because they were afraid of it? Can you think of people who died just before or just after they retired?
✦ Can you think of an oldster neurotically obsessed with illness and pain, who whined and fretted constantly?
✦ Can you think of a senior who spent most of his or her days home alone with the TV?

We all have fears about retirement and about growing old. And we just have to look around to know that retiring and growing old are empty and unhappy experiences for a great many people. Senior citizens commit suicide at more than twice the rate of the general population. They are more often clinically depressed and consume more anti-depressants than any other age group. Sociologists tell us that about two-thirds of the senior population age at an accelerated rate, becoming prematurely old and prematurely dead. Roughly half that number are distressed or unhappy, with a similar number reporting experiences ranging from moderately happy to so-so.

Now consider more hopeful role models. See if you can locate examples of the following in your memory store:

✧ Can you think of an oldster who was joyfully eccentric, feisty, and playful and who knew practically everyone?

✧ Can you think of an older person who seemed to get bigger with the passage of time?

✧ Can you think of someone who took forever to get old?

✧ Can you think of an oldster who was joyfully active, eccentric, feisty and playful; someone who knew practically everyone?

Your hopes for retirement are also based firmly in reality. Seniors are over-represented among the happiest people in North America. About one-third of the senior population report feeling the happiest they have ever felt at any time in their lives.

Social scientists say that the happiest seniors are also the healthiest and longest-lived. What's more, there is strong evidence that vitality and longevity in later years are not so much a source of happiness as a consequence of feeling happy, fulfilled, and connected. (We'll be looking at this research in more detail in Chapter One.)

Why is it that the second half of life turns out so well for some and so miserably for others? Society's prescription for happiness in retirement is that you should have long-lived parents and save a big pot of money. All the research to date on successful aging points to a very different conclusion: *Wealth and genetics are both minor factors in determining who is happy and healthy later in life.*

Contrary to the blandishments of the just-be-patient types, that same research also suggests that the pathway to happiness later in life begins long before your sixty-fifth birthday. *There is strong evidence, in fact, that enjoying a happy freedom now is the absolute best training you can give yourself for feeling happy and free later in life.*

Scouting the Future

It sometimes feels naively arrogant to be writing a book about the second half of life at age fifty-two — a bit like a thirteen-year-old trying to write about adolescence. So let me say up front, I am not an "expert." I wrote this book for me as much as for anyone else. It is the book I wish someone had given me on my fiftieth birthday — or, better yet, the day I turned forty.

I think of myself as a scout. I may still be on the edge of this delightful new territory, but, being a thorough and careful explorer, I've taken the time to pick the brains of a great many people more familiar with the territory than I. There are millions of people across North America who have already said "Enough Already." Some broke free in the last few years; others, decades ago. And while we boomers will undoubtedly want to break free in our own way, I've gained insight talking with people who have already broken trail for us.

I've also studied carefully what social scientists tell us about who is happy in the second half of life, and why. In addition, scattered amongst that huge pool of literature written for seniors by seniors are a great many asides about what seventy-year-olds wish they had known at fifty.

I have had some opportunity in the past few years to begin exploring personally the freedom that is possible in the second half of life, and I am able to report directly on the kaleidoscopic deliciousness of that experience. I like to think that my novice status has some advantages in that I can ask questions that will resonate for many of my peers. If you, the reader, receive even a fraction of the value I received from researching and writing this book, you're in for a treat.

As a counsellor, I've always needed to bring my self into my work to be effective with people. Something of the same process happens in my writing. Whenever I come upon some general principle or strategy in my research, I try it on for size. Can I feel this principle at work inside me? Do I see it reflected in the people around me? How do my friends feel about it?

I invite you to do the same thing. All the personal examples I include in this book have come either from people I know directly or from friends of friends. The steps to breaking free in the second half of life are neither obscure nor exotic. You can see them in the people around you. I share my inner process in part because I see that the most difficult challenges of breaking free have nothing to do with external circumstance, but rather with our internal impediments. You will see that too. As Pogo would say, "We have met the enemy, and they is us."

Claiming Your Freedom

The first step in breaking free is to understand more clearly what shackles us. "Freedom from" precedes "freedom for." In Chapter One I will examine the false freedom of traditional retirement and show why it's not worth waiting for. In Chapter Two we will explore what I call the OverWorld, the normalized insanity that has most North Americans overspent, overworked, overstressed, overtired, and overweight by mid-life.

The second step in breaking free is to motivate yourself by building a positive vision of how freedom would enable you to better meet your most basic needs, both now and in the future. Chapters Three, Four, and Five deal with the three fundamentals that people must address in order to feel free, fulfilled, and happy all through the second half of life: purpose, connection, and challenge.

The third step in breaking free is to establish the conditions of freedom. Chapter Six is about finding a new path to financial freedom, while Chapter Seven is about putting work in its place. Then, if you're going to get a flying start on the second half of life, you'll need to clean up whatever baggage remains from your time in the OverWorld. Chapter Eight looks at recovering your balance and getting a life; Chapter Nine at cleaning up any unhealthy lifestyle habits.

In choosing to claim your freedom now, rather than waiting to "retire," you will need to swim against the cultural mainstream. Try to do that on your own and you will likely fail, so Chapter Ten offers a bonus challenge. It suggests how to find allies and support for breaking free, and how to make your freedom potent in the larger world.

There's an inherent paradox in writing a how-to book about breaking free because real freedom involves discovering your own unique path. Accordingly, I present my steps to freedom not as prescriptions, but as passports. Passports that I believe can lead you to new and exciting destinations. Enjoy the journey.

A Postscript: Dreamy Wisdom

Last night I had a dream that woke me up laughing.

In the dream I was watching a football match. The quarterback was the old man of the team. There had been speculation for several years that each season would be his last, but he was still out there, still the anchor to his team. At half-time I wandered down to the sidelines to chat with him.

"How do you keep such energy through a whole game?" I asked.

He talked first about pacing himself and about the need to keep his cool when the game was going against him.

Then he said, "At the end of the first half, when we go to the dressing room, I let go of whatever happened in the first half. The other team can come back completely different after the break. They'll be pumped or mean or have a whole new game plan. Even your own team can surprise you. If you're expecting the second half to be like the first, you'll get caught off guard.

"There's only one way to think of it," he said, shaking his fist for emphasis. "The second half is a whole new game."

CHAPTER ONE

The False Freedom
of Traditional Retirement

Retirement is the Promised Land we are entitled to if we survive forty years of labour and strain. Yet many of us boomers feel underwhelmed and ambivalent about the "freedom" retirement offers.

The start of breaking free is to understand the limits that traditional retirement seeks to impose upon you. I call them the Terrible TOOs of retirement. Retirement comes TOO late, TOO suddenly, and TOO expensively. As a life script, retirement is TOO limiting. Finally, our idea of what it means to be old is itself TOO old.

Too Late

Have you ever wondered how the standard retirement age of sixty-five was selected? Why sixty-five and not fifty-five or seventy-five? The age was chosen way back in 1889, when German chancellor Otto von Bismarck was under pressure to develop an income support program for German workers too old to work. Unfortunately the German treasury at the time was nearly bankrupt. Bismarck's solution: Set the bar high. Sixty-five was chosen as the age of eligibility because at that time most German workers died well before their sixty-fifth birthday. Furthermore, those who worked until they were sixty-five were usually so worn out that they also soon died and thus made only modest demands on the public purse. There was nothing magical about the age of sixty-five. It was chosen arbitrarily based on what a financially strapped German treasury could then afford.

In the years since, state and private pension schemes have been built around an assumed retirement age of sixty-five. It remains an arbitrary number, and the original reason it was chosen — that you as a retiree wouldn't live long enough to be expensive for the pension provider — is hardly the most compelling argument for waiting until you are sixty-five to change your relationship with work.

Not far from where I used to live on Denman Island, off the east coast of Vancouver Island, there's a small hill in the road. A few years back, Helen Dale, administrator for the town of Comox, BC, was bicycling up that hill with her husband when she had a massive heart attack and died, right there on the side of the road. Helen was sixty-two. She was planning to retire about the time I write this in 2004.

Bismarck's "solution" is still with us. Between their fiftieth birthday and the time they turn sixty-six, one in ten North American working women will die. For men the odds are even worse. One fifty-year-old working man in six will die before his sixty-sixth birthday. Couples often have elaborate retirement dreams. If you and your spouse are both fifty, there's one chance in four that one or both of you will be dead before you reach age sixty-six. If, as often happens, the man is older, the odds get even worse. If a woman's husband is seven years older than she is, the odds rise to one in three that one or both of them will die between her fiftieth and sixty-fifth birthdays.[1]

Bismarck's solution also continues to keep pension costs down because of the price in wear and tear that full-time work exacts from middle-aged bodies. If you wait till you are sixty-five to stop your full-time work career, there's a good chance you will drive into retirement with little tread left on your tires. With much of your natural vitality gone, your ability to remain healthy in your post-work life could be compromised.

On the other hand, you have a say in the lottery of mortality. If you reduce your workweek sometime in your fifties, you can reduce that wear and tear. You can also use some of your new free time to improve your lifestyle in ways that will revitalize your health, both now and later.

The rewards of doing so are much greater now than they were in Bismarck's day. Back then, people died of old age in their fifties and sixties. Sixty-year-olds who took good care of themselves might eke out a few more years of life in declining health. Today, most of the people who die before their sixty-fifth birthday are otherwise youthful and healthy individuals who have been struck down by heart disease or cancer. A healthy lifestyle can cut your risk of dying of either by two-thirds or more. Tip-toe past those two great killers and you are likely to enjoy decades of health and vitality.

Another problem with an arbitrary retirement age of sixty-five is that it may not fit your particular life situation. If your spouse is older, you may want to leave the workforce when he or she does. Your body may send insistent health warnings that it is time to do something different. Grandchildren arrive when grandchildren do. If you want to be an active, involved grandparent, you'll need to do it on their timetable, not Otto von Bismarck's.

Your readiness for something new in life will come when it comes. If the thought of working full-time till your sixty-fifth birthday is enough to make you immediately depressed, perhaps you need to take your work life off "Otto"-pilot.

Oh, and by the way, if you're prepared to wait until you retire to have your freedom, I should warn you that Newsweek is already predicting that "in 15 years the normal retirement age will be 70 or more."[2] The age at which Americans can collect Social Security has already begun an upward slide from sixty-five to sixty-seven. Canadians can still collect the Old Age Pension at sixty-five and a reduced Canada Pension Plan as early as age sixty, although policymakers are quietly considering higher entitlement ages for the not-too-distant future.

Too Sudden

The second problem with traditional retirement is that it starts so suddenly. For forty years, paid work is the skeleton around which you build your life. Then, poof, in one day you're expected to make the transition from having most of your life structured for you to suddenly managing all of your time, every day, for the rest of your life.

Longer workweeks and dual-earner households have made work even more primary to the North American lifestyle and have aggravated the trauma associated with sudden retirement.

I think we've all met someone who has retired, yet keeps showing up at the old workplace looking like a lost puppy. Most people can also think of workmates or family friends who retired and were dead within a year. They so much didn't know what to do with themselves that they died of shock.

Many retirees go through a three-stage process upon retirement. First there's a honeymoon period of one to six months. Retirees sleep in late, read books, travel the country in an RV, visit grandchildren, and/or socialize with friends. It has the feel of a long, relaxing vacation.

The second stage is often a gathering crisis of purpose. It may include a crisis of boredom and isolation. If the retirees' work roles were a major part of their persona, they may also feel a loss of identity. The distress in this period can be intense, resulting in health problems, clinical depression, even suicide.

Over time, as retirees develop new relationships, new activities, and new purposes, they usually view retirement as a blessing again. Those who have managed only to "keep busy" tend to experience merely a reduction in distress, while those who feel connected, involved, and useful will typically report their post-career years as extremely happy.

Is there a value in having retirement be this sudden, overnight change of life? Does it need to be this way? Some people relish the opportunity to completely remake their lives all at once and thrive on the challenge. For most of us, though, it is gentler and healthier to let go of employment gradually, to "get a life" before letting go of paid work entirely.

When work dominates too much of a person's time for too many years, a kind of wage slavery can set in:

✧ The skills to manage your own time — to know what you want, to trust your own sense of what is most important, to juggle and balance competing demands on your time, to show initiative in making your wishes a reality — can become unfamiliar. It requires a certain courage, confidence, and self-knowledge to be the CEO of one's own life.

✧ The number and intimacy of your non-work friendships may diminish over time. Connections with extended and even immediate family may become distant and prickly. Gradually you become isolated.

✧ Non-work skills and avocations may be lost. Longstanding dreams and pleasures may be neglected so long that they fade from memory.

✧ Links to the community can become attenuated. As an example, you may still go to church regularly, but the richness of connections there — choir, church social events, friendships with church members — may become impoverished.

One of the most damaging results of wage slavery is that money becomes the final arbiter of value. In his thought-provoking book *The Gift,* Lewis Hyde argues that, in most societies, freely given gifts, rather than business transactions, are the natural basis for human relationships, and the constant trading of *Homo economicus* has diminished us. Where North Americans engage in the "business" of living, other cultures relate to life as an art form or a sacred journey.[3]

If you watch young children, you will see that most of what they do, they do for the pleasure of the activity itself. While adults have learned to trade time for money, to see life as a series of trades where "I do A to get B," children are more open to a world of immediate pleasures and freely given gifts.

For wage slaves, money often determines and measures value. Only that which is done for money is seen as having value. Later in life, if people haven't learned to work for love, they have far fewer avenues available for finding a sense of place and purpose in the world.

Those who enter retirement suddenly from unbalanced lives dominated by work often lack the skills, connections, interests, and non-work passions to make a successful transition to a satisfying post-employment lifestyle. They are likely, by default, to continue some of the worst aspects of wage slavery in their post-career life.

If a person's lifestyle at age sixty-four consists of work, sleep, shopping, and television, the default template for life in retirement will be to sleep, shop, and watch TV. Indeed, the average senior in North America watches forty-five hours of TV a week. Jack Nicholson gives a chilling portrait of this aimless, lost life in the movie *About Schmidt*.

One of the unstated assumptions about traditional retirement is that you will work full-time until the day you retire. However, once your children leave home, you could probably find ways to cope on a part-time income. Even if you are not able to leave the paid workforce completely until your pension kicks in, you do have choices about *how much* to work in the interim. Working less than full-time could give you a chance to learn the skills you will need later in retirement, as well as the opportunity to enjoy *now* many of the pleasures we normally associate with retirement.

Too Expensive

If I were designing hell, if there were O'Hara's Inferno in place of Dante's Inferno, many of the world's investment advisors would end up down in the seventh circle of hell. Way down there, even below advertising psychologists. Why? Because your average investment advisors make their clients slaves to work.

How's that? First, investment advisors typically don't help you reduce the excessive and addictive spending that makes it difficult to save for retirement without becoming a card-carrying workaholic. Then they recommend that you aim for a retirement income big enough to meet those same excessive expenditures, plus more for travel blowouts. Finally they scare people with "what if" scenarios about inflation and termites eating your house, saying, "Really, you should add 50 percent to what you think you need, because once you stop work, that's it, you're stuck with what you've got."

Your typical retirement planner wants a working couple to have a million dollars in investments and own their own home outright before they retire. That's several times what you need! Surely investment advisors could spend at least a little time helping people consider what trade-off they are prepared to make between time and money.

Corporate pension plans are often similarly extravagant. A typical private pension plan will provide 70 percent of your best year's salary after thirty-five years of service. Add Social Security to that in the US (in Canada, CPP and OAP), factor in tax deductions for seniors, and many retirees end up with an after-tax income near that of their best working years. This at a time when they no longer have children or a mortgage to support, when they can get seniors' discounts on a wide range of products and services, and when the considerable expenses of working life have disappeared.

If you can unhook yourself from this all-the-bells-and-whistles model of retirement, you may be able to free yourself from the need to work for money at a much earlier age — and be able to work less in the meantime, too.

Too Limiting

Our supposed compensation for decades of an all-work-and-no-play lifestyle is an all-play-and-no-work bonanza. That may sound like an attractive proposition from the trenches of a work-dominated life. However, in practice it often leads to a life that is limiting and sterile. Retiring becomes a retreat from the world.

Retirees in North America are given social permission to behave like over-aged children with no responsibilities, no demands placed upon them, nothing they owe the world. They're free to retreat to seniors' communities and fish, golf, watch TV, or play bridge, all day, every day.

In this model of retirement, decades of labour have earned retirees the right to permanent and selfish leisure. Life is one long vacation; you don't have to do anything you don't want to do ever again. It's a hands-off-the-wheel approach that leads many retirees to withdraw from life and neglect even the basics of good health.

The permanent vacation model of retirement is a holdover from a different era. A hundred years ago, average life expectancy in North America was less than fifty years. Even in 1935, when Social Security first became available in the United States, average life expectancy was only sixty-two years. If you hung on long enough to retire at age sixty-five, retirement was usually a brief and precious twilight. "Relax and take it easy" was probably good advice.[4]

Today, the typical senior will spend decades in retirement. In recent years a number of prominent researchers have been involved in major research projects to determine who is happy and healthy later in life, and why. The results of that research are clear: the permanent vacation life script is not conducive to either health or happiness for today's seniors. The happiest and healthiest seniors, it turns out, are anything but retiring.

Successful Aging

John Rowe and Robert Kahn's book *Successful Aging* is based on a ten-year, $10 million MacArthur Foundation project involving sixteen researchers. The project consisted of dozens of studies that examined large populations of seniors to winnow out the minority who aged slowly and gracefully, and then determine what distinguished these "Successful Agers" from the general population of seniors.[5]

David Snowdon's *Aging with Grace* presents the results of a study of 678 older Catholic nuns whose physical and mental health was carefully tracked over a fifteen-year period. All of the nuns were regularly interviewed about their daily routine and attitudes.[6]

George Vaillant's *Aging Well* offers a third window on this question of who ages slowly and well. Vaillant presents data from three longitudinal studies of human development: the Grant Study of 268 male students attending Harvard University; the Glueck Study of 456 men selected as non-delinquent boys from inner-city Boston; and the Ternan Study of 682 Californian women chosen as schoolgirls.[7]

Rowe and Kahn, Snowdon, and Vaillant all found a subset of the senior population that aged more slowly. The researchers agree that while it certainly doesn't hurt to have parents who live a long time, behaviour and not genetics is the best predictor of health and happiness later in life.

Kahn and Rowe are the most emphatic in their findings. They observe that a significant subset of the senior population has health profiles more typical of people ten or twenty years younger. These Successful Agers typically live ten to twenty years longer than the general population, and even though they live longer, they are marginally less likely to end their days infirm or senile. What's more, members of this healthiest group of seniors are also the happiest people in their age cohort.

In their discussions of the aging process, Rowe and Kahn feel compelled to distinguish between "usual" aging and necessary aging, arguing that most North Americans age at an accelerated rate because of lifestyle decisions, not due to any fundamental constraint of biology.

For many people, the prospect of adding twenty years to their allotted span is initially exciting, but then sobering, because they imagine those years tacked on at the end, when they're frail and sickly. What the MacArthur study discovered was that the extra years are inserted in the middle. *It was as though some people took twenty-five years to age from fifty to fifty-five, and thereafter maintained a body age twenty years younger than their calendar age.*

David Snowdon found that because his entire study group of nuns tended to live in ways that slowed the aging process, they formed a good case study of Successful Agers in and of themselves. He reports that "the risk of death in any given year after age sixty-five is about 25% lower for the School Sisters of Notre Dame than it is for the general population of women in the United States." As evidence of the longevity of his sample group, Snowdon includes a group photo of seven nuns over a hundred years of age, all living at one convent.[8]

George Vaillant noticed that each of his three study groups contained a subset of people who aged much more slowly than their cohort. Vaillant devised a series of health and happiness scales with which to analyze his data. By comparing the behaviour of one-quarter of the subjects in each study group who had the highest overall health and happiness scores (Happy-Well) with that of the quarter of subjects who had the lowest scores (Sad-Sick), Vaillant shows that his Happy-Well subjects shared attitudes and behaviours not common among the Sad-Sick.

All three sets of researchers stress that health and happiness tend to go together in the second half of life. While it may be somewhat easier to feel happy if you are healthy, the researchers found that the causal connection seems to operate much more powerfully in the other direction: happy people stay healthy and live longer. Separate research with a Mexican-American population has since corroborated that being happy cuts by half a senior's risk of dying in any given year, and also halves the annual risk of becoming disabled.[9]

The researchers all note that people who age slowly and gracefully tend to share four characteristics:

✧ They take reasonable care of their physical health.
✧ They keep learning and challenging themselves mentally.
✧ They are well-connected in their communities, with friends of all ages, and they continue to make new friends.
✧ They have some sense of purpose or passion in life.

In short, Successful Agers are *engaged* rather than retired. They are physically and mentally active. They are involved in their communities. They make themselves useful.

The life habits that make some of us happy, healthy, and durable later in life rarely begin late in life. Regular exercise is the most important lifestyle habit seventy-year-olds can have if they want to remain healthy, yet only 20 percent of seniors exercise regularly. What's the best predictor of who will exercise at age seventy? Regular exercise at age fifty.

George Vaillant's data supports this early-is-better theme. In all three of his study groups, participants had a much greater chance of being in the Happy-Well group at age seventy-five if at age fifty they didn't smoke, didn't abuse alcohol, got some exercise, and weren't overweight.[10]

The skills and habits of friendship and community involvement may be perfected later in life, but the foundation for those skills is usually laid down at mid-life, decades before a person begins collecting a pension. *If you want to be happy for the rest of your life, start now.*

Too Old an Old

The final problem with traditional retirement is that many people associate retirement with getting old, and much of our thinking about getting old is itself old and out-of-date. The scientific community's view of the aging process has undergone profound changes in recent years, but the general public's perceptions of aging haven't caught up.

In decades past, science promulgated a view of aging as a universal process of inexorable decline. No more. When scientists talk about the necessary losses of aging, they are much more restrained than they once were. The necessary declines are relatively minor and include modest losses in acuity of vision, hearing, taste, and smell. Memory losses are gradual and can be offset by training. The immune system's ability to protect against infectious diseases and cancers very gradually diminishes. We spend less time in deep sleep. Connective tissue gradually loses its elasticity. We heal more slowly. All of these changes are typically slow and modest in those who stay physically fit and mentally active.[11]

All of our body systems gradually lose reserve capacity as we age, but reserve capacity is just that: reserve. It is surplus to what we normally need. So long as we still have *some* reserve capacity, its loss has minimal impact on how we feel from day to day.

Scientists will allow that in the final few months of life there is often a steep and abrupt decline in both physical and mental health, but this generalized breakdown of all the body's systems should be seen as part of the dying process, not as aging per se.

What has caused science to retreat from the idea of aging as a universal process of inevitable decline? One thing that has made science more optimistic is that aging keeps changing. For the past hundred years, average life expectancy in North America has been rising by about three years per decade. Not only are human beings living longer, but we are staying youthful longer too.

Most gerontologists would now go so far as to say that we should be very careful in using the past as a guide to the future. If, for example, you were to base your expectations of aging on grandparents fifty years your senior, statistically speaking you would be short-changing yourself of between ten and fifteen years of youthfulness and longevity. Scientists are expecting our generation will live longer, and be youthful longer, than any generation before us.

The other thing that has changed science's attitude to aging is the recognition that early research on the aging process was flawed: flawed in the sample populations chosen, flawed in control group selection, and flawed in the testing instruments used.[12]

Let's start with who was studied. If you wanted a captive audience of old people to study, what would be your easiest source? Nursing homes, of course. Decades later, researchers realized what a skewed initial sample population this was. First of all, most people don't go into nursing houses until they've already begun that short, steep slide at the end of life. We now also know that old-style nursing homes, by doing absolutely everything for their patients, inadvertently accelerated the aging process. So researchers chose as their first subjects the least healthy of seniors, in the worst possible setting.

When researchers began looking at aging losses through the life cycle, they initially began measuring subsequent generations against one another. So in 1960, say, they would take basic measurements on physical and mental abilities for a group of forty-year-olds, compare them to groups of fifty-year-olds, sixty-year-olds, seventy-year-olds, and eighty-year-olds and — lo and behold — they found a steady decline in physical and mental abilities across that forty-year age span.

The losses scientists measured were considerably smaller than previous research had predicted, which eventually clued them in to the dangers of using nursing home residents as a sample population and to the existence of that abrupt decline at the end of the life cycle. Nonetheless, scientists confidently announced that it was all downhill after age thirty, and that became the prevailing wisdom about aging.

This model of aging really began to come unglued when researchers did ten-, twenty-, thirty-, and forty-year follow-up measurements on the forty-year-olds they had initially tested. What researchers found was that the average declines measured were all much smaller than previous cross-generational studies had indicated. How could this be? they asked. Eventually they realized that because life expectancy in North America has been increasing by about three years per decade, each earlier generation studied had more of its members in the period of steep decline that precedes death, and measuring generations against each other exaggerated the losses associated with aging.

The other thing researchers began noticing was how differently we age. Forty years on, a fairly homogenous group of forty-year-olds had turned into a group of eighty-year olds vastly different from one another. It was simply not accurate to talk about a universal aging process. In fact, there was a substantial subset among the eighty-year-olds who showed only trivial declines in physical and mental abilities forty years later, which inspired the successful aging research.

Scientists also realized belatedly that some of the standards they had used to measure intelligence though the life cycle were not age-neutral. IQ and memory tests were deliberately designed to measure reasoning abilities separate from culture and separate from what can be learned through experience.

However, while knowledge gained from life experience did not help people get a good score on such tests, practice did. The type of mental tasks used for IQ and memory tests are not common in daily life, except in one place: school. Not surprisingly, the more years that had passed since a person was in school, the lower that person would score on memory and IQ tests.

This flaw became obvious when researchers began giving seniors practice before they took IQ tests. Researchers at Pennsylvania State gave hundreds of sixty- to eighty-year-olds standard IQ tests. Participants were then given five to ten training sessions on reasoning problems over several months and retested. The improvement in their IQ test scores was approximately equal to the loss of IQ that science, up until that point, had considered to be the consequence of the aging process.

Researchers then did a comparable study using standard memory tests before and after participants had had thirty memory-training sessions. Once again, with the kind of practice that most students get in school, memory facility showed a huge improvement. "After thirty sessions of memory training every one of those sixty-seven- to seventy-eight-year-olds was able to repeat at least thirty words and strings of digits as long as forty in the correct order, though they were presented only once."[13]

When they say that the necessary losses of aging are minor, scientists are not implying that the aging process is always slow, but rather that the speed at which we age is more a function of behaviour than biology. If, as a senior citizen or even as a middle-aged person, you stop using your body, it will begin to atrophy. Muscle mass will disappear. Bones will weaken. The cardiovascular system will lose fitness. If you stop using your mind, your memory and reasoning abilities will diminish. All of these losses will be a result of disuse, not of aging.

At any time in the second half of life, if you live in ways that leave you lonely, bored, or feeling useless, depression is the likely result. Tiredness and lack of energy have always been the classic symptoms of depression. Depression will also lower your resistance to infectious disease and increase your risk of heart disease and cancer. Once again, however, these unhappy outcomes are not the result of aging, but of behaviour.

The bottom line on all this is if you are feeling tired or less mentally sharp, now or at any time in the next few decades, you need to understand that it's not about "getting older." It may be about being too stressed. It may have to do with lack of sleep. It may have to do with a lack of physical fitness. It could be the result of an undiagnosed illness. It may be a result of depression. It's not about getting old.

The other important truth that science has uncovered is that our expectations of aging have a huge impact on the aging process. A major study reported in the August 2002 issue of the *Journal of Personality and Social Psychology* found that holding a positive attitude towards the aging process can extend your lifespan by an incredible 7.5 years.[14] So, before you go any further, please take to heart this summary of what I've said so far: *If past trends continue, scientists expect the boomer generation will live longer, and age more slowly, than any generation before us. And if you behave like today's Successful Agers do, you can look forward to even more years of robust health and vitality.*

It's Time To Retire 'Retirement'

The whole modern idea of "retirement" is flawed — in how late and suddenly it starts, in how expensive we've made it, in the passive lifestyle it promotes, and in the outdated concept of aging it reflects. It serves most people to junk retirement, both the word and the concept. In its place I would suggest the term "financial independence."

People are financially independent when they are free of the *need* to work for money. In the past the term was mostly used to describe rich young people who might or might not work for money, who often felt a certain noblesse oblige to do good works. But let's face it, if you are free of the need to work for money, you are rich. And if you're smart, you'll find some way to make yourself useful. Better yet, you'll do this early in the second half of life, while you're still young.

CHAPTER TWO

The Insanity
of the OverWorld

For so many North Americans, it's all "over" at mid-life. They are overworked, overspent, overstressed, overtired, and overweight. To break free of this culturally normalized overburden, it is necessary to first see it clearly.

Our culture is like a river that wants to carry us along in its flow. We can choose to sail our own little boats across the river's flow or even to work our way upstream. But whenever we're not paying attention, the river will take us where the river is going.

The fact that you have picked up a book on breaking free in the second half of life probably means that you can feel the pull of the larger culture, and you don't necessarily like where it wants to take you. This may not be the first time you've wanted to chart your own course. Perhaps you have already steered at least partway clear of the OverWorld described below. Please give yourself credit for whatever success you have had in escaping the collective craziness and, as you read, appraise what shackles remain to be broken.

Overworked

Work, contrary to the brave predictions of a generation of futurists, has increasingly come to dominate the lives of most North

Americans. In twenty-first-century America it seems you can have a job or a life, but you can't have both.

It wasn't supposed to be this way. Technology was supposed to create an Age of Leisure in the twenty-first century. What isn't generally understood is that technology did deliver. Productivity in North America has more than doubled since 1948. As Juliet Schor points out in *The Overworked American*, "We could now produce our 1948 standard of living (measured in terms of marketed goods and services) in less than half the time it took that year. We actually could have chosen the four-hour day. Or a working year of six months. *Or, every worker in the United States could now be taking every other year off from work — with pay*" (italics in original).[1]

When we moved to having two breadwinners per family, we could have had abundant leisure *and* a modestly higher standard of living. As a society we had that choice, but we chose instead to go in the opposite direction. Overwork and burnout are now so prevalent in North America as to seem normal.

If we had gone overnight from the lifestyle of 1954 to that of 2004 there would have been stunned shock, followed by rioting in the streets. Three things have happened in the past fifty years to put most working people under thumbscrews.

The first is the shift to the dual-earner family. Married women in the 1950s had a full-time job: they raised children, cooked, and kept house. When they went out into the paid workforce, two adults had to cover three jobs between them. At first the "Second Shift" (Arlie Hochschild's wonderfully ironic book title) was carried mostly by women. Over the past thirty years, as feminism has worked its way through the culture, some men and women have slowly been finding more equitable ways to share home and parenting duties. But that third job hasn't disappeared. Two people are still doing three jobs.

Second, contrary to the expectations of the futurists, there's been a gradual but cumulatively large increase in working time. The average North American's work year increased by 199 hours between 1973 and 2000. *Time* magazine reported in 2003 that 80 percent of men and 62 percent of women in the United States were putting in more than forty hours per week on the job.[2] Almost 40 percent of American and 25 percent of Canadian workers now work fifty hours per week or more.[3]

Finally, we have seen a gradual but relentless intensification of work. Across North America, millions of workers have been laid off over the past thirty years. New technology only took over part of the laid-off workers' load; the rest is now carried by the remaining workforce. Millions of North American workers live in a Dilbert doublespeak world where "multi-tasking" means you are doing three people's jobs. Cell phones, pagers, home computers, and wireless Internet mean that work invades more and more of what used to be private time and space.

Working people in continental Europe work an average of 350 hours per year less than we do in North America. Even the Japanese now work less than we do. Where the typical European worker is guaranteed five weeks' annual vacation time by law, American employers are not required to provide *any* vacation time to their employees. In America you are "free" to work every week of the year. Fully 25 percent of American workers took no vacation days last year. Canada has a legal minimum of two weeks' vacation pay per year, but only the extra pay is mandated by law. Employers can require employees to work right through their vacation as long as they are paid vacation pay on top of their regular earnings.

The rest of the world thinks we North Americans are somewhere between sick and crazy — that we don't have nearly enough time for fun in our lives, and that too little leisure makes us lousy spouses, inadequate parents, poor friends, and uninformed citizens.

If a typical US worker were to drop back to a European work year, he or she would need to take all of July and August off work, with pay. Any vacation or holiday days previously scheduled for July or August could then be taken as additional paid time off in September. Wouldn't that change your summer? Is it any wonder the Europeans pity us?

The Time Famine of Modern Life

As an advocate for shorter work times, I have tried to practise what I preach, and for much of my work life I have succeeded in keeping my workweek between twenty and thirty hours. From time to time, however, I have made forays into the world of full-time work — most recently while completing this book.

Whenever I worked full-time I found it easy to lose my balance. Perversely, I would watch more TV as my workweek got longer. I'd spend less time with friends, be less involved in my community. It was easy to get sedentary, to put on extra pounds. Sensuous pleasures of all kinds became less available. I felt tired more. There'd be a background feeling of low-level irritability and impatience. Eventually it became so normal that I'd no longer notice I was quicker to anger.

Always, the more I worked, the more I would spend. I would buy more prepared foods, eat at restaurants more, pay other people to fix or clean instead of doing those tasks myself. I would reward myself with expensive toys. I would comfort myself with "treats" of unhealthy food. Even the government took more in taxes when I worked more.

I recognize all those symptoms, to one degree or another, in most of the full-time workers I see around me. I can also see that when you live without balance for long enough, you no longer experience the deprivation that results.

So if you are working full-time, and particularly if you and your spouse both work full-time, *consider whether doing so may be costing you more than you know.*

What do I see in the typical full-time worker's lifestyle? Tiredness is so chronic one forgets what it feels like to be really rested.

Impatience, crankiness, a susceptibility to colds and flu, and loss of interest in sex all become "normal." Your job gets your best; the rest of your world gets the leftovers.

People try to explain away the price they pay for a work-obsessed lifestyle. They say that tiredness is a function of aging, lack of interest in sex is caused by changing hormones. When people put on extra pounds, they blame their lack of discipline around diet and exercise. When they lose touch with friends, it is because they didn't "make the effort." When their spouse becomes distant or prickly, they blame themselves for not paying enough attention.

Various other activities get squeezed out over time: fun with friends, family time, community activities, citizenship responsibilities, even hobbies. Dual-earner spouses often don't get enough couple time to maintain a sense of intimacy.

Non-career competencies may disappear after years of neglect. Fixing one's car, playing a musical instrument, cooking or sewing skills, all can become unfamiliar under the North American regimen of industrial-strength overwork.

By default, TV becomes a major avocation. It's not that TV has gotten better over the years. It's just that, at the end of a long workday, people are too pooped to do more than zone out with the box. They blame themselves for that, too.

The flip side of increasing overwork is rising unemployment. In my previous book, *Working Harder Isn't Working,* I showed how official government statistics systematically undercount the true number of jobless people in Canada and the US by about half.[4] Though governments are loath to admit it, about one working person in eight in North America is unemployed. When polled as to why they are not taking vacations, an increasing number of Americans report they fear being targeted for layoff if they take vacation time or limit work hours to the time for which they are paid. Mass unemployment thus serves as The Enforcer for endemic overwork.

Overspent

By the beginning of 2004, the average American household carried US$20,000 in short-term debt, double what it had been ten years previously. Mortgage debt rose 50 percent in the same period, as millions of Americans borrowed against the equity in their homes. The average US household carries more than US$80,000 in consumer and mortgage debt.[5] Canadians are not far behind. The average Canadian household now carries CDN$67,000 in debts — up sharply in the past five years.

What Juliet Schor calls the Work-and-Spend lifestyle causes families to live with almost no safety margins: "Indeed, 60 percent of families have so little in the way of financial reserve that they can only sustain their lifestyles for about a month if they lose their jobs. The next richest 20 percent can only hold out for three and a half months."[6]

The individual results of the overspent lifestyle are destructive enough. It gets downright ugly when we look at the collective outcome. Filmmaker and author John de Graaf calls our collective malady "affluenza," which he defines as "a painful, contagious, socially transmitted condition of overload, debt, anxiety and waste resulting from the dogged pursuit of more."[7]

Our North American proclivity to work too much, spend too much, and waste too much has huge consequences. Here are a few of the shocking statistics from de Graaf's insightful and funny book *Affluenza:*

✧ In each of the past four years, more Americans declared personal bankruptcy than graduated from college.
✧ We now have twice as many shopping centres as high schools.
✧ Since 1950, Americans have used up more resources than everyone who ever lived on earth before then.

- Average Americans now spend six hours a week shopping and only forty minutes playing with their kids.
- Including secured apartment dwellers, residents of gated communities, prison inmates, and people with residential security systems, at least a fifth of America now lives behind bars.
- Industry moves, mines, extracts, shovels, burns, wastes, pumps, and disposes of four million pounds of material to provide one average middle-class family's needs for a year.[8]

How can it be that we're working so much, earning so much, and yet as a society we are spending it all and more? What's going on that the more we have, the more we seem to need? How is it that "more" never seems to be "enough"?

Net Worth and Self-Worth

The philosophical underpinnings of America's runaway consumption are two-fold. First, we have a core belief that more will make us happy. A corollary is the idea that "successful" people have more than "losers" do — i.e., that my worth as a person is evidenced by my possessions. The obvious link between these two ideas is that it's easier to feel happy with and about yourself when you feel worthy.

In her groundbreaking book *The Overspent American*, Juliet Schor gathers together some fascinating research on the relationship between money and happiness. It turns out the connection between how much money people earn and how happy they are is remarkably weak.[9]

Even in retirement, the connection between wealth and happiness is tenuous. A 1996 Australian study found no relationship at all between money and happiness for retirees across an income range between AUS$10,000 and $100,000 (the income equivalent of US$8,000 to $80,000 or CDN$10,000 to $100,000).[10]

Here's a trick question for you: What annual income would you need to earn to be really happy? Do you have a dollar figure in mind? How big is that number compared to your current income?

Sociologists have been conducting polls on happiness for a long time. The question I just asked you is one that sociologists frequently ask in polls. Most people, when asked, can name a dollar amount that they think would make them really happy, and it's generally about $20,000 per year more than what they are making, *at all income levels.*

At all income levels. Does that little phrase make you suspect there's something not quite right here? The people who are making $20,000 more than you are still think *they* would need another $20,000 to be happy. And even those rich folk making $20,000 more than the people making $20,000 more than you still think that with just *another* $20,000 they could be really happy. Suddenly the stairway to happiness looks more like a treadmill.[11]

Average real incomes in America have approximately doubled in the past forty years. If "more" had the power to make us happy, how do we explain the fact that Americans' self-reports of happiness peaked in 1957 and have been sagging ever since?[12]

Though money by itself doesn't bring happiness, social scientists have found a strong relationship between what they call "relative wealth" and happiness. To determine relative wealth, researchers asked questions designed to help their subjects identify who they considered to be their peers. Researchers then measured the income of that reference group compared to the subjects. Subjects who were richer than the people they considered to be their peers were generally happier than average. Respondents who were poorer than their identified peer group were typically less happy.[13]

So, for example, if you were an investment banker making $250,000 per year, and you considered your peers to be bankers with million-dollar salaries, not only would you rate yourself as less happy than average, but people who knew you well would rate you as unhappy. On the other hand, if you were a shop clerk making $25,000 a year, but most of the people you saw as your peers made less than that, usually you would be happier than average.

Why has happiness in America been declining? Fifty years ago, most people saw their neighbours, friends, and co-workers as peers. On that basis, most people had income levels close to that of their reference group.

In recent decades, Americans have shifted to a wannabe reference group, made up of the people they *wish* were their peers. About one-third of Americans now consider the richest 6 percent of the population as their reference group. *Increasingly, the people Americans see as their peers are television characters rather than real people.*[14]

One of the interesting revelations in the research on what people thought made them happy was how sensitive that research was to the wording of the questions. When researchers asked their subjects to list what made them "happy," the answers were usually heavily laden with consumerism: a new car, the vacation in Maui, a raise at work. But when researchers changed the language slightly and asked subjects when they felt contentment, peace of mind, or satisfaction with life, the subjects began talking about the joys of loving relationships with friends and family, the pleasure of serving some larger purpose, the excitement of learning and personal growth. Such responses made it clear that the things which provided short-term happiness "highs" were quite different from what gave respondents lasting satisfaction.[15]

Here perhaps we have the link between relative wealth and happiness. If people saw themselves as having more than enough, they put their energy into enjoying what they had rather than into worrying about what they didn't have. They put their time and energy into friendship, family, and community — the activities most effective at generating lasting satisfaction.

However, if people saw themselves as not having enough, they typically invested vast amounts of time and energy into earning more and into shopping for badges of status. Getting and spending, they laid waste their days.

There is such a strong relationship between overwork and overspending that it is often hard to determine which is chicken and which is egg. Overspending eventually locks us into overwork, which in turn makes us overstressed, overtired, and eventually overweight. In Chapter Six we will explore ways to escape the awful treadmill of "I owe, I owe, it's off to work I go."

Overstressed

The time famine of modern life leaves many North Americans racing through their days, never quite catching up, like the White Rabbit of *Alice in Wonderland,* forever lamenting, "I'm late, I'm late." Task overload is a huge source of stress; so is the social isolation that typically results from overwork. Both stresses carry huge health risks.

What is less well understood is how effective stress is at draining the pleasure from life. To help you understand why this is so, I will need to take you on a short tour of the physiology of both stress and emotion. This will also show you why chronic stress is so hard on your health.

The body has two identifiable types of stress response: alarm and vigilance. Both responses are biologically ancient, more suited to the Stone Age than the Computer Age.

The alarm stress response is triggered by immediate emergencies. It prepares the body to fight or flee, whether the threat is a hungry tiger, a forest fire, or — in today's world — an angry spouse and a looming deadline at work.

Alarm stress reactions are orchestrated by the release of the hormone adrenalin. Every body system goes into its own emergency drill when the adrenalin siren goes off:

✧ The heart pounds faster so that it can pump more blood to the muscles, and blood pressure skyrockets.

✧ Sugar pours into the bloodstream so it is instantly available to provide energy for fight or flight.

✧ The chemistry of the lungs changes, and breathing speeds up in order to bring more oxygen into the body.

✧ Blood is diverted away from the digestive system and to the muscles to provide energy for fight or flight.

✧ The blood supply to the skin is reduced so the person won't lose as much blood if he or she is cut or injured, and the skin goes partly numb.

✧ Endorphins, natural morphine-like chemicals, are released into the blood, creating a euphoric energy rush and enabling the body to keep moving even if it's hurt.

✧ The pupils get bigger to let in more light and increase visual acuity; hearing also becomes more sensitive.

✧ The large muscles of the body go tense, ready for battle, but also creating a natural armour that makes the body harder for a predator to rip open. (Remember what I said about the Stone Age!)

During an alarm reaction, the body is preparing itself for an anticipated physical challenge. It conserves its resources by neglecting activities that don't have immediate survival value. All of the body's maintenance and repair activities shut down temporarily. The digestive system slows to a halt; food in the stomach starts to rot.

This emergency response system is designed to be used only occasionally. If the human body spends too much time in an alarm state, the body's routine maintenance doesn't get done. If tiny tears in the small blood vessels aren't repaired in a timely fashion, they will become larger rips that bleed into and damage surrounding tissue. If the immune system cells that hunt down and destroy cancer cells are out of action too long, cancerous growths can become established. If digestion stops for too long, dangerous toxins are produced.

The vigilance response is a second stress response designed to provide the body with the staying power it needs to survive in marginal conditions like a famine, drought, or blizzard — or, in today's world, a 900-calorie diet or an impossibly large project at the office.

The vigilance response is orchestrated by a slow and steady release of the hormone cortisol, causing the following reactions:

✧ The person becomes irritable and hyper-alert.
✧ The body stores fat whenever it can.
✧ Salt is retained and blood pressure rises.
✧ Fat and cholesterol levels in the bloodstream increase.
✧ The stomach secretes more gastric acid.
✧ The sex hormones are suppressed.
✧ More blood platelets are produced.
✧ The heartbeat slows.
✧ The immune system goes into overdrive.

The vigilance response makes the body use food, water, and salt more efficiently (this increase in metabolic efficiency explains why crash diets lose their effectiveness over time). It also temporarily gives increased protection against infectious disease and faster healing of injuries. Unfortunately, the things your body does to make your heart more efficient also make it far more vulnerable to what cardiologists call "sudden-death" heart attacks. As well, the immune system can become exhausted; once the crisis is over, you get sick.

The Joylessness of Stress

In order to see how stress affects our ability to feel good, let's take a short detour that begins with what may sound like a naive question: What is an emotion?

When we have an emotion, a symphony of neural and chemical

messengers go out to the body. They originate in the hypothalamus, a part of the brain so ancient it is nicknamed the "lizard brain." Feelings go way back in our evolutionary history; even reptiles display emotions akin to fear and anger.

The link between an emotional response in the body and our conscious experiencing of it is indirect. Most people can think of times they've broken something or sworn at someone and had it be their first clue that they are really angry about something.

What we call an emotion is technically a synesthesia — a combination of several separate, discrete processes that the brain puts together so firmly we experience it as one gestalt. The sensation of taste is also a synesthesia. Consider the taste of chocolate, for instance. When we "taste" chocolate, several things are happening at once. Various chemical receptors in the nose are stimulated by aromatic gases coming off the chocolate. The sugar sets off sweetness receptors on the tongue. The jaw muscles send signals to the brain, which the brain decodes as a particular texture. Caffeine and various endorphin-like chemicals from the chocolate enter the bloodstream from the salivary glands, creating a contented sensation. The brain combines all these separate things going on in the body into one gestalt, which we identify as a "chocolate" taste. Synesthesias tend to collapse if any of the pieces are missing. I know, for example, if I have a stuffed-up nose, chocolate becomes underwhelming. Without the aroma, the richness of the "chocolate" experience disappears.

What are the elements of the synesthesias of emotion? Each emotion includes a unique set of components: a particular set of hormones in the bloodstream; a specific form of breathing; a particular way of holding the chest muscles; a certain sensation in the belly; specific skin sensations, especially in the face and around the eyes; and finally, a particular way of holding the large muscles of the body.

The body combines this diverse set of elements into one package, which we experience as a particular emotion. As with chocolate, take one or two elements out of the synesthesia and the gestalt collapses. If, for example, you clamp down tightly with your chest muscles, you can choke off almost any emotion.

Let's play a little game for a minute or two. I'll list a number of emotions. For each one, quickly identify for yourself where and how you feel it in your body. Here goes:

✧ Shame. Anxiety. Sadness. Anger. Grief. Embarrassment.

Now try:

✧ Bliss. Joy. Contentment. Wonder. Curiosity. Playfulness.

When you thought about where in your body you felt the various emotions, which were subtler, the pleasant emotions or the unpleasant ones? Unpleasant feelings are generally warnings that something is awry in us or our world. Those warnings need to be fairly strong and insistent to ensure they are not ignored.

Pleasant feelings have more the quality of rewards. They do not need to be as dominant. In fact, it has probably served the survival of the species to have them easily pushed aside when danger threatens.

Consider for a moment what happens to your capacity for pleasant emotions when your body is in an alarm response:

✧ **Your lungs are pumping harder.** That "on guard" reaction doesn't leave much room for anything else. The choppy breathing of panic will register, but the openness in the chest associated with joy is buried.
✧ **Your bloodstream is full of adrenalin.** Adrenalin is so loud it tends to drown out the more subtle hormones associated with any emotion other than fear or anger.
✧ **Your digestive system is shutting down.** Forget about the warm fuzzies in the belly that come with contentment.
✧ **Your skin is partly numb and drained of blood all over your body, including your face.** Forget that openness

around the eyes that comes with wonder. Forget the tingly skin of joy. There's no room for them.

✧ **The big muscles of your body are all tense.** Forget the bounciness of playfulness. Forget the relaxed muscles of bliss. Neither is available.

The vigilance stress response undercuts pleasant emotions in similar ways, although not as completely as the alarm response. You end up with wimpy, *Reader's Digest* condensed versions of feeling good — like the taste of chocolate with a head cold.

Pleasant emotions that rely on stimulation of the sympathetic nervous system — surprise, excitement, and sexual arousal — are less affected by stress, but even these pleasant feelings are sabotaged by high levels of alarm or vigilance.

Everything I've said about emotions goes double for sensual pleasures. Whether we are talking about the taste of food, the cosy warmth of a wood fire, or the excitement of sexual arousal, stress reactions — especially strong ones — sabotage and interfere with all those experiences. Though stress makes sight and hearing more acute, the stressed brain tends to filter out sensory signals not related to our survival needs, so beautiful sights and sounds are ignored. If stress is long-term and chronic, a person literally forgets what it feels like to really feel good.

I'd like you to do a little exercise that may help you personalize what I have said about stress and pleasure. First, take a minute to settle back and relax. Draw a few deep breaths. Now close your eyes and remember what it was like the last time you had a relaxed, leisurely vacation — at least ten days, and preferably three weeks or more. A do-very-little vacation as opposed to a busy one.

Remember the sights and sounds of that time. Remember who you were with. Remember how you felt. Remember the physical sensations, how your skin felt, how your body felt. Remember the taste of food. Remember the emotional tone of the time.

What was that like? When I've done this exercise in workshops, most people report that at such times all their senses seemed more intense — colours were brighter, tastes were richer. Sensual, erotic, and emotional experiences were stronger and more intense. Often we attach the magic of such times to the place, or to the person with whom we shared the experience, rather than recognizing how a relaxed state opens us to feeling good in all sorts of ways.

I would like to make the subversive suggestion that the pleasure, the sensuousness, the vibrancy of that vacation you remembered is your birthright. It's how we human beings are meant to live most of the time. And it's how you could live more of the time if you were willing to say "Enough Already."

Overtired

Sleep deprivation is endemic in North America. We sleep an average of seven hours and twenty minutes a night, which is sixty to ninety minutes less than most of us need for optimal performance in the world.[16]

Sleep deprivation is sometimes simply a consequence of the task overload of modern life. When there aren't enough hours in the day to have both a job and a life, we steal time from sleep. Just as often, though, sleep deprivation is caused by people having difficulty falling asleep or staying asleep.

As the human body ages, hormonal changes cause it to spend less and less time in the deep sleep that is most restorative. Because we sleep less deeply, we are more prone to being wakened by background sounds, the movement of our partner, or even by our own dreams.

By middle age, lighter, more fragile sleep makes us more vulnerable to the "overs" of modern life. Long work hours can leave us with too little time for exercise. Exercise, particularly earlier in the day, is a proven aid to good sleep. Being overweight makes exercise more difficult and makes sleep apnea more common.

Sleep apnea, aside from whatever health risk it poses, tends to disrupt sleep. Stress hormones make it hard to fall asleep and easy to waken in the middle of the night.

Sleep deprivation is not just an issue of feeling cranky and fatigued. Sleep is when the body does much of its maintenance and repair work. Dreams are when the mind does its emotional house-cleaning. We feel rejuvenated after a good night's sleep because our body has had a chance to flush out any buildup of toxins, bacteria, and viruses. Without sleep to "knit the ravelled sleeve of care," the body ages more quickly. The Harvard Nurses' Study, a longitudinal study of 71,000 female health care professionals, found that nurses who got six hours' sleep per night or less were one-third more likely to have heart attacks than nurses who got eight hours' sleep. Even getting by on seven hours' sleep increased nurses' risk of a heart attack by one-sixth.[17]

Are you tired of feeling tired? Perhaps it's time to say "Enough Already!".

Overweight

Sixty-four percent of American adults are overweight and 23 percent are obese. Obesity has increased by 74 percent since 1991. Obesity, implicated in 300,000 deaths per year, now rivals smoking as the leading cause of death. The epicentre of the obesity epidemic comes at mid-life. It's almost cliché to have a spare tire around your middle in middle age.

Being overweight gets more dangerous as we get older, particularly when it is combined with smoking. Being overweight past the age of forty knocks 6+ years off your expected lifespan. Smoking also knocks 3+ years off your life expectancy. But if you're an overweight smoker past the age of forty, your life expectancy is reduced by more than thirteen years![18]

Why are North Americans so overweight? Usually we blame ourselves, but we get lots of "over" help. Overwork means we're often too busy to exercise. The vigilance stress response causes the body to become metabolically more efficient. And, perhaps most importantly, the time famine of modern life has created dietary norms that make it easy to put on weight.

The Lure of Convenience Foods

In a lifestyle starved for time, we have tended to want food that meets three criteria: it tastes good, it's quick to prepare, and it won't spoil. How do you make prepared food that won't spoil? Vitamins, minerals, food enzymes, and essential oils all tend to make food go off in flavour or spoil quickly, so they are removed from most prepared and convenience foods. Usually it is also necessary to strip the fibre from foods in order to remove the essential oils.

Making food that won't spoil has several consequences. When you eat food stripped of vitamins, minerals, and essential oils, your body is left vulnerable to various deficiency diseases. The body will also tend to crave more food — even when it has eaten too many calories — because it still needs to obtain missing nutrients. Foods without fibre lead to constipation, colon cancer, and blood sugar crashes.

Unfortunately, when you take the vitamins, minerals, essential oils, and fibre out of food, you also remove most of the flavours, aromas, and textures that make food attractive. How do you make this boring food something a person would want to eat? Just add salt, sugar, and fat.

Back in the Stone Age, humans living far from the sea had a hard time getting enough salt in their diet to replace the salt lost through sweating. A craving for salt encouraged our ancestors to seek out rock salt deposits and naturally salty foods whenever they could.

Very few naturally sweet foods are poisonous. Because sugar tastes good, it encouraged prehistoric humans to eat foods that wouldn't kill them. Sugar in whole fruits and vegetables typically came surrounded by vitamins, minerals, protein, and fibre, so the craving was also nutritionally sound.

Back then, having some fat on your body was a form of life insurance against periodic famine. Wild animals were far less fatty than their modern domesticated counterparts, so dietary fat was often in short supply. Because fat tasted good, humans were encouraged to stock up on it whenever they could.

Nature still equips us to crave salt, sugar, and fat. Unfortunately salt, sugar, and fat are now added to thousands of prepared foods. We eat so much salt it has created an epidemic of hypertension. Sugar is added as pure sugar, devoid of nutrients and fibre. Sugar without fibre is absorbed by the digestive tract so quickly that the body has to convert it to stored fat to keep blood sugar levels from going too high. Dietary fat is an efficient form of calorie storage — one pound of lard has as many calories as forty pounds of lettuce — which makes it easy to take in too many calories when you eat prepared foods with added fat.

The result is that if you eat a lot of prepared foods and/or restaurant meals, you are almost certainly eating too much salt, too much sugar, and too much fat. You're likely also deficient in your intake of vitamins, minerals, essential oils, and fibre. You are at increased risk of heart disease, diabetes, cancer, and hypertension. For many people on a diet of prepared and convenience foods, the only way to avoid becoming heavier is to feel hungry all the time.

It may seem odd to think that there is a lack of "freedom" attached to convenience foods. After all, such foods are supposed to free us from the "drudgery" of cooking. Anyone who is required for health reasons to cut down on salt, sugar, and fat will initially feel that change as a severe *loss* of freedom.

What we must remember is that convenience foods taste good mainly because of habit. Within a matter of months on a new diet, new habits make new foods taste good. Whole foods offer the palate a richer bouquet of flavours and textures than do refined foods. Whole foods tend to provide better nutrition and more vitality. When you're not starved for time, cooking is a pleasure, not a chore.

The bottom line is that the time famine of modern life makes it hard to live and eat in ways that will keep you slim, healthy, and energetic.

Escaping From the OverWorld

In the 1960s, all the futurists predicted that technology would bring an Age of Leisure. Without thinking, we took their *predictions* as *promises*. Certainly, if you had asked any of us then what we thought our lives would be like at fifty, we would have described a rich, adventurous freedom. Our future was the Jetsons. If you had told us then that the future was Dilbert and Dogbert, we'd have said, "That's crazy!"

It is crazy. And if you're fed up being a part of the insanity of the OverWorld, there is a way out. It doesn't involve waiting to retire at age sixty-five or seventy. It's more fun than that, and it starts now. The freedom the futurists promised us is indeed available, but it won't come for those who sleepwalk into the second half of life. In the next seven chapters I will examine seven steps to freedom. If you want your freedom, you must choose it *now*.

CHAPTER THREE

Know Why You Are Here

After the last chapter you're probably clearer on what you want freedom from. In the next three chapters you'll have the opportunity to begin creating a positive vision of where freedom might take you, both now and later.

As a way to structure the envisioning process, I want to look at three fundamental human needs that are often inadequately met at mid-life: purpose, connection, and challenge. As it happens, these three needs become even more crucial the older we get, so addressing them now can help make the whole of the second half of life a more satisfying experience.

As you read through the next three chapters, don't attempt to create a game plan for the rest of your life. Rather, allow yourself to build some fantasies, to create some excitement for yourself about what a life of freedom could mean to you. Doing this will generate the energy and motivation you're going to need for the hard work of establishing the conditions for freedom in your life.

The way to enjoy these chapters is to read them as if you were already free of the constraints of the Overworld. Read them as if you already had the freedom to go where your heart leads you. Later, when you've created more time and space in your life, you may want to come back to these chapters and use them as a tool for action planning. For now, focus on the feelings.

The Primacy of Purpose

Let us begin with the issue of purpose. There's nothing more necessary for feeling fulfilled and happy in the second half of life than knowing why you are here. This is not to say that all or even most of the pleasures of the second half of life come from purposeful activity. People who report feeling a richness and abundance in the second half of life often experience it across several domains. Much of their enjoyment comes from rich human relationships and from having time to relax and play.

However, people who lack a clear sense of purpose are more likely to feel lost, useless, and unworthy. When such feelings are present it is easy to isolate yourself, easy to feel that even fun activities lack meaning. Purpose is a compass and a foundation upon which the other pleasures of life rest.

Purpose is also incredibly idiosyncratic. For one person, water-colour painting may be the most important, most exciting thing in the world; for someone else, painting is just a pastime that staves off boredom. It isn't even necessarily a matter of talent or proficiency. You can be really good at something, but if there's no passion, it does not confer meaning.

Purpose is paradoxical in that it can take us deep inside ourselves and, at the same time, far out into the world. Philosopher Sam Keen says it well:

> The central repression in contemporary Western culture is the need for purpose, meaning, and a sense of the sacred. There can be no cultural and spiritual renaissance unless millions of individuals make the repressed questions a matter of ultimate concern: "What is my purpose? What is the meaning of my life? What is sacred for me?" But our time demands more than this of individuals. Today, we need to forge a link between solitude and political-communal engagement. Those who are willing to explore their spiritual unconscious must emerge from the womb

of privacy and from the sanctuary of religion and give themselves to the heroic task of creating a new form of political life.[1]

While we often speak of purpose as though it were one thing,
most of us have several purposes in our lives that, between them,
create a sense of knowing why we are here. On the other hand,
it's not like you can just gather purposes in a shopping cart until
you have enough. A satisfying sense of purpose is seldom
achieved without a clear central or core purpose.

The Mid-life Opportunity

We often imagine that retirement is when a person may need to
wrestle with issues of purpose and identity, but the evidence
suggests that purpose issues frequently emerge at mid-life.

George Vaillant uses psychologist Erik Eriksen's life-cycle task
model to frame three developmental tasks for young adults. He
believes that to become a mature, fully functioning adult, a
young person must achieve a sense of identity, develop a capacity for intimacy, and experience a measure of success in the
world of work. Young adults receive strong social support and
validation to do this developmental learning in three basic arenas: family, home, and career. As a result, these three arenas
often provide them with a strong sense of purpose and meaning.[2]

By mid-life, our relationship with all three arenas may be
undergoing profound change. Children grow up and leave home.
The need to "nest" (to buy and outfit a home with furnishings
that express our identity) may largely be met. And a career may
also go through profound changes.

People who have stuck it out in boring or hated jobs because it
was what they needed to do to provide for a growing family may
find the old job is intolerable once the kids leave home. Other
people find they have done what they wanted to do in a particular career, and staying longer feels like putting in time.

Then there are all the people who, like it or not, are thrust into a new relationship with work. The relative stability of North American unemployment rates obscures how much "job churning" has happened in recent years. Every year, several million people lose their jobs and must find new ones. More often than not those new jobs have less status and pay less than the old ones did.

Second Adolescence

Those who initially experience these changes in home, family, and career as losses may try, in various ways, to hang on to the old. Parents may become clingy and intrusive with their grown children or may pressure their children to produce grandchildren. A couple may compulsively redecorate. There usually comes a point, however, when change is experienced as liberation rather than loss.

We always have choices. A thirty-five-year-old with young teenagers can go back to college or trek the Himalayas in search of enlightenment. Once the kids have left home, however, those choices become ever so much easier. We have more space and time to think about what our needs and choices are, fewer responsibilities, and fewer people who must live with the consequences of the choices we make. Sometimes even before the children have actually left home we can see ahead to a new set of choices for ourselves, and we're ready for the new life almost before the new life is ready for us.

Abigail Trafford, in her book *My Time: Making the Most of the Rest of Your Life,* refers to this experience of new freedom as a second adolescence.[3] The world is suddenly full of choices. You could move to a new place. You could go back to school. You could start a new career. You could go off to Africa as a volunteer.

Second adolescence is like the first in that people are free to focus again on their own needs rather than those of dependent children. There can be a desire to experiment, not just with new activities, but also with new identities and new roles. There can be fear and doubt commingled with excitement and a sense of adventure.

There are also some significant differences. Where society sets out a series of supported roles for young people, society is much less clear about what are worthy purposes for a fifty-three-year-old. In second adolescence we often have greater resources than we did the first time round: more personal and professional skills, more financial resources. We may have a better idea of who we are and what we want.

Not everyone reaches second adolescence at the same age. Some people at forty-five are finished raising their children, others are just beginning, and some never procreate. For people who have spent their thirties and forties raising children, career may be a brand-new and totally absorbing source of purpose at fifty. Nonetheless, most people at some point during the mid-life decades go through a "changing of the guard." Old purposes fade or come to completion, and a new purpose must be found.

Career, home, and family are all big, powerful purposes that invest young lives with meaning. As those purposes lose their primacy, it opens up a hole — sometimes a big hole.

When the hole is still small, you will probably experience it as a liberation. As the hole gets bigger, any of a number of less pleasant feelings could emerge. You could feel antsy or restless, impatient, depressed, like a has-been, lost, confused, anxious, or fearful. If you experience any of those feelings, it may be time to take a closer look at the issue of purpose.

New Purposes Take Time

New purposes take time to develop. My own research talking with people about the changes that come at mid-life mirrors the patterns described by Abigail Trafford in *My Time* and Jacqueline Blix in *Getting a Life:* It can take two to five years for new purposes to become clear.[4]

Before new purposes are fully formed, most people need to go through a process of casting about. They'll do some experimenting and try on ideas for size. Usually there's a blind alley or two and a period of vagueness before a new direction really comes clear. Typically there's a certain amount of confusion and uncertainty, even a feeling of being lost. If any or all of these things are happening for you, relax. It's normal.

A couple of ideas follow from the twin realities that living without purpose can be unpleasant, but new purposes take time. The first is that it's useful to think about what you want to do next in your life *before* the old purposes lose their lustre completely. The second is that it doesn't serve most people's interests to leave the workforce overnight unless they have some clear idea what comes next. If you know that you're going back to school for an architecture degree, great — go for it! If you have no idea what comes next, do yourself a favour and work part-time until you have at least some vague idea about where you're headed.

That being said, it is sometimes necessary to let go of the comfortable and the familiar to open the space for new purposes to form. Until recently, being an activist has been a strong part of my identity. A good chunk of my friendship circle was made up of activists, and many of the social events that brought me into contact with those friends were centred around protest and information campaigns to influence governments to behave more sensibly and morally. In recent months my interest in these kinds of activities has dried up suddenly and completely. It's not that I now see these activities as valueless — they are needed as much now as they ever were. It's just that my energy is being drawn someplace else.

I don't yet know what my new focus will be and where it is going to take me. I know that finishing this book comes first. I know that when this book is done I want to be involved in some sort of local community group that encourages and supports people to live in more environmentally sustainable ways. I know I will be volunteering with the new Habitat for Humanity affiliate in Courtenay, helping low-income people build their own homes.

I have a strong hunch that if the Habitat model could be melded with environmentally sustainable building methods, some powerful synergy could result. Do I have a timeline? No. Do I know who my partners in this dream will be? Not yet. Do I know what the new group will look like? Not at all. Can I guarantee that some other purpose won't overtake this one before I get there? No, I can't. (Remember what I said about how new purposes usually start by being vague? This is vagueness!) Still, that's all the direction I need to feel excited rather than distressed about the future.

Finding New Purpose for Yourself

Finding new purpose is more of a journey than a task.

In my work counselling clients over the years, I have found a number of questions helpful for choosing and recognizing new purpose. Such questions seem to work best when they are asked as invocations. Don't gnaw on them with your busy brain. Ask a question as if you were fishing; wait for the answer to surface.

Where Is Your Juice?

For many people the term "purpose" may convey the idea of being useful or dutiful, of doing what we're "supposed" to do. But purpose has more power as an experience than as a concept.

What activity puts juice and excitement in your life? When do you feel most alive? (Adrenalin highs that come from putting yourself in danger or attempting to do the impossible don't count.) When do you feel like you are most yourself? "I ____, therefore I am." Do you have a love or passion for something that creates a bond with others who share a similar passion? If there's nothing like that in your life now, has there been in the past?

Is there a particular activity or relationship in your life with such power that time seems to stop when you're doing it? Mihaly

Csikszentmihali calls this a state of "flow."[5] Flow can produce transcendent states: intense concentration without effort; feelings of oneness; time speeding up, slowing down, or seeming to stop. It's usually a good clue you're onto something hot.

Less important than what is done is how it feels. For some people, gardening is a way to fill time, a way to keep busy. For others, gardening is a simple pleasure that grounds them in the world. Then there are the people for whom gardening is a passion. The garden is where they feel most alive, most themselves. Their strongest connections with other human beings involve a shared love of gardening. Even their sense of the sacred involves the metaphor of the garden.

Our society tends to overlook and undervalue non-economic activities. If what has juice for you is art, music, poetry, singing, or dance, the larger world will tend to trivialize and dismiss it. You don't need the world to understand or value your passion. What you need is to own and honour what has juice for you.

What Choices Have You Hidden from Yourself?

Our lives are full of choices at mid-life. If you believe that the best of life is over and all that remains for the second half of life is amusements and pastimes, it almost certainly means that you have choices you're not letting yourself see.

Sometimes, as uncertain young people starting out, we rationalize our choice of direction with the lie that our path is the only real path, or that our path is superior to all other paths. If sometime in the past you convinced yourself that business executives — or mothers — are the only really important people in society and that every other job is second-best, that arrogance will come back to haunt you in the second half of life. Let go of the lie.

If you are feeling grey and blasé at fifty, you may need to pick through the trash-heap of all the ideas and dreams you've ruled out of consideration:

✧ If you were less "realistic," what would you do?
✧ If you were twenty again, what would you do?
✧ If you were totally without fear, what would you do?
✧ If you could be guaranteed that your friends wouldn't laugh at you, what could you maybe, possibly, be interested in doing? (Remember to wait for the answer.)

Before I leave this question, I'd like to take a minute to address a particular subset of the male population. Over-represented among the seniors who commit suicide are men who had positions of status and power during their work lives. It is not unusual for such men to sink into a deep funk once the initial elation that follows retirement is over. The common complaint of such men is that they now feel "useless" and "irrelevant."

If you're one of those men, or think you could become one, I need to talk to you. Because your life may be at stake, I'm going to take a risk and be fairly blunt: You probably won't feel better until you stop lying to yourself about the nature of your problem, which has nothing to do with either uselessness or irrelevance.

I know that if you are free of the need to work for money, there are literally thousands of choices available to you. You can choose to work on whatever issue you believe is most crucial to the future of our world, and you can probably carve out a niche for yourself that puts all of your best skills to good use.

I suspect the losses you are feeling stem from something else. You're unlikely ever again to have as much public attention and status as you had when you were a big mucky-muck. You probably won't have fawning subordinates stroking your ego. It's unlikely you'll have the same opportunity to wield power over others as directly or crudely. Those are very real losses.

However, slitting your wrists over those losses is like the aging Hollywood starlet pouting because she's no longer offered ingenue roles. She turns down' meaty, complex parts playing mature women — Oscar-worthy roles — because she wants to be the centre of attention playing some beautiful young innocent.

If you have propped up your sense of self-worth all these years with external crutches of attention, deference, and top-dog status, you may need to spend some time learning how to generate your sense of worth internally. That's not an easy task, but it can be done. In the meantime, get on with the job of making yourself useful and relevant.

What's in Your Shadow?

Is there a road not taken in your life? Is there some area of your life where you feel incomplete? Is there some realm of life that you avoided, not because it lacked interest to you but because you felt too clumsy, too inept, or too embarrassed to go there? Are you ready to go there now?

The reward for going into the shadow is that it gives us the intensity and excitement of beginner's mind. There can be a real specialness and power in going to those places which have held longing or fear for a long time. It can bring a sense of fullness and completeness to life. (We'll explore this topic further in Chapter Five.)

What Is Your Response Ability?

For most of us in our twenties, thirties, and forties, family is a major sphere in which we feel useful. Dependent children are a particularly rewarding focus for our usefulness because they "need" us. Then they grow up. To feel useful in the second half of life, you may have to extend your circle of caring. Purpose requires needs.

The idea that once you are financially able to leave the workforce you have paid your dues and owe the world nothing is a recipe for isolation. One of my favourite definitions of responsibility is that it is our "response ability." How able are you to respond to the needs of others? That's your response ability in the world.

In a world of global corporate capitalism, many of the world's problems seem overwhelmingly large. Doing nothing makes a person feel powerless, that he or she doesn't matter. We need to scale down from the general and the abstract to the small, the specific, and the concrete. Theodore Roosevelt put it succinctly when he said, "Do what you can, with what you have, where you are."

Take climate change as an example. Three separate computer models of global climate change have indicated we could be less than twenty-five years away from the point where we have so destabilized the planet's ecology that climate change will spin out of control regardless of what humans try to do to stop it. Climatologists the world over have been shocked at the extraordinary number of extreme weather events the world has seen in the past ten years, and the World Meteorological Organization is now saying that either we've been having an extended run of extremely bad luck or global warming is happening even faster than scientists had predicted.[6] In February 2004 a leaked report from the Pentagon, not usually thought of as an extremist environmental organization, warned that by 2020 the world could see catastrophic flooding, mass starvation, widespread war and global chaos if global warming was not brought under control soon.[7]

It can be tempting, in the face of such a huge impending catastrophe, to slip into denial, to say, It really isn't happening. Scientists or the government will find some kind of solution. Fixing it is not my job. "Somebody" should do something about this, but I can't.

It is true that the changes in lifestyle required if we are to forestall ecological collapse are enormous. But if I allow myself to become overwhelmed and retreat into denial, I am part of the problem. The enormous task of reinventing a sustainable society is made up of ten thousand smaller challenges: pick one. Each of those ten thousand tasks may also feel too big for you to make a difference on your own, but all that means is that your first job within that task is to find allies.

What Is Your Highest Purpose?

Bob Buford includes one of my favourite George Bernard Shaw quotes in his popular little book *Half Time:*

> This is the true joy in life, the being used for a purpose recognized by yourself as a mighty one; ... the being a force of nature instead of a feverish, selfish little clod of ailments and grievances, complaining that the world will not devote itself to making you happy.[8]

Buford argues that the challenge of the second half of life is to let go of worldly success as a goal and to find a life task of "significance." The philosopher Jacob Needleman echoes these sentiments with his observation that when twenty-five-year-olds make fame and fortune their life's focus, it can have a stirring boldness; when a person of fifty can find no higher purpose, it is vaguely pitiable.[9] If your best and wisest self were to speak, what would it ask of you? Where would your soul lead you? What legacy would you like to leave the world?

Twenty years ago I did a fire-walking workshop. At the end of it, our instructor, Tolly Burkan, warned us that we would feel fear more often after the workshop. I thought, "This is nonsense, Tolly. I just walked on hot coals — nothing scares me now." But he was right. The reason I felt scared more often was because I allowed myself to really want something.

I allowed myself to want something that was bigger than me. I decided that I was fed up with living in a society where almost everyone I knew was either overworked or unemployed. What I wanted was to live in a place where there was a job for every person who wanted one, where we shared the work and shared the leisure. Wanting that required me to do a whole slew of scary things I'd never done before. I had to find a sponsor. (Thank you, Joan, for believing in me.) I had to learn to write funding proposals. I had to learn how to hire staff and supervise them. I had to learn to write bylaws and recruit board members for a new organization. I had to learn to speak to large groups of people, to write media press releases, to write books. I was scared a lot more often than I had been prior to walking on hot coals, and I felt *alive*.

Here's the most powerful antidote to fear I know: Allow yourself to care passionately about something that's bigger than you are. The wanting will carry you past your fears. Pick something big enough and worthy enough and you'll have a job for the rest of your life.

What wants to get into your heart? Is there some issue or problem that keeps getting under your skin? What is the one thing you would like to see happen in the world? If you could have one wish fulfilled for your local community, what would that be?

We all have pet peeves and pet causes. If you have a full-time job, your pet causes may come out in "somebody" statements. "Somebody really should do so and so." Once work no longer dominates your life, that "somebody" could be you. Are you prepared to be a somebody?

"Somebody" jobs can be a job and a half. Usually there's no ready-made job to step into. You have to write the job description, recruit your co-workers, and create your workplace before you can start the job. The bigger the job you take on, the more help you'll need to recruit.

There are so many needs out there, you cannot possibly act on every "somebody" urge you feel. But sometimes a "somebody" urge is too hard to resist. If you see a particular need with clarity and poignancy, it may be because that particular job has your name on it.

Is It Time to Experiment?

As mature adults, we may criticize young people who change their minds too often while trying to figure out what to do with their lives. It's true that it's not satisfying to be a permanent dabbler. It's also true that young people often give up before they've given something new a fair trial. However, with those two caveats, experimenting is a powerful way to find out what feels right.

Sometimes the only way to get where we want to go is by successive approximations. Even an experiment that is a stone-cold failure can help by telling me where my purpose isn't and is a step on the road to warmer, warmer, *HOT*.

Is there some wish or dream you've had for a long time? Perhaps years ago you received counselling and found value in it. Maybe you felt drawn to become a counsellor yourself. Perhaps you are still curious but not sure that you would enjoy it or have any aptitude for it. Maybe you need more information before you can know whether this is the path for you. Volunteer with a local crisis line. Then you'll have some idea whether it's a dream worth pursuing.

Small experiments often work better than big ones. It may be difficult or scary to move into a new arena. Small steps get your foot in the door. If the experiment doesn't work out, your investment was small too.

There's a point in Lewis Carroll's *Alice in Wonderland* when Alice asks the Cheshire Cat which way she should go. The Cat replies, "That depends a good deal on where you want to get to." When Alice replies that she doesn't know, the Cheshire Cat responds, "Then it doesn't matter which way you go." Going any direction will give you more information than being stuck in not knowing.

If you want a workbook to help in the process of finding new purpose for yourself, I recommend Richard Leider and David Shapiro's *Repacking Your Bags*. Bob Buford's *Game Plan* does something similar using an explicitly Christian focus.[10]

What Would You Do for Love?

What do you care about so much that you'd do it for free?

One of the basic assumptions of North American society is that the more something costs, the more valuable it is. What does it mean, then, if I work for nothing? Does it mean my volunteer work is useless or less valuable than paid employment?

One skill that's useful to acquire in the second half of life, if you haven't learned it earlier, is the ability to work for love. Our society does a better job of expecting and supporting women to work for love than it does men, so this is a particularly crucial skill for men to master.

Many people do not have to learn how to work for love per se. They may love their jobs and express caring for the world through their work. However, they do need to learn how to unhook from money as a validation or justification or motivation for work. That's important, because when love alone is sufficient incentive to put you to work, you have a hugely expanded range of choices. All of the paid work choices that were available to you before are still available. In addition, there are literally thousands of volunteer opportunities to choose from. And if you don't like any of the existing choices, you can always create your own volunteer position. With such a huge range of choices, you can choose work that feels important, useful, and relevant. You can choose something with challenge and excitement. You have the freedom to go beyond the constraints that so often limit what a person can do in a paid job. As a volunteer, you can even set your own hours.

Do you want to make a difference in the world? I believe that it is easier to make a difference in the world working for love than for money. Why is that? Because for most paid work you can name, if you got hit by a bus tomorrow, someone else would soon be doing your job. With paid work, it's the money that gets the job done. Making a difference in paid employment is limited to how you do your job better than any likely replacement would.

With volunteer jobs, on the other hand, there's a good chance if you don't do the work, it won't happen. What you do for love adds a good to the world that likely wouldn't happen without you.

Becoming an Elder

The older you get, the more likely it is that you will find the developmental tasks of young adulthood have ceased being sources of meaning in your life. We have seen how long it can take to discover new sources of meaning, so it's not too early to begin thinking about how you plan to be useful twenty years from now. Once you leave the paid workforce, it becomes crucially important to know why you are here and to have a clear sense of your place and value in the world. Robert Kahn and John Rowe identify "active engagement with life" as the single characteristic that best typifies the Successful Agers they studied. David Snowdon believes that a major reason his nuns outlived most American women was that a life purpose of service to others — lifelong service — was a central organizing principle for them.

George Vaillant goes even further. At the beginning of this chapter I outlined the three developmental tasks Vaillant identifies for young adults. He also posits three developmental tasks for the second half of life:

✦ **Generativity.** Learning to be an unselfish guide to the next generation, to be in relationships where one cares for those younger than oneself and simultaneously respects the autonomy of others. Generativity can mean serving as a consultant, guide, mentor or coach to younger people. Generativity can be being a leader or a community-builder.
✦ **Keeper of the Meaning.** Being someone who helps in collecting, recording, and passing on the wisdom, values, and history of the larger society in which one lives.
✦ **Integrity.** Developing a detached wisdom, which includes honesty, self-acceptance, and character.[11]

Though Vaillant found that all three of these developmental tasks had the power to create meaning, fulfillment, and a sense of purpose for his study participants, mastering the task of generativity was clearly the most crucial. "Generativity provided the underpinnings of successful old age," he writes, adding that the good effects of feeling involved and useful had wide-ranging impacts in participants' lives. "In all three of our samples the mastery of the Eriksonian task of Generativity was the best predictor of an enduring and happy marriage in old age." For the study's women, success at generativity was the best predictor of whether they reported attaining regular orgasm.

Taken together, Vaillant's three developmental tasks also constitute a good summary of the skills needed to perform the traditional roles of an elder. Today we live in a society with a propensity to marginalize its old people. But for 99.9 percent of human history, the longer people lived, the more they were at the focal point of their clan or tribal circle — as a repository of tribal history, as a trusted arbitrator of disputes, as a guide and mentor to younger generations, as the matriarch or patriarch who could lead gently but wisely. The older you got, the more useful you became, the more important and valued your ideas were, and the wider your circle of connection became.

One way we might describe Successful Agers is to say that they are people who have managed to become elders in their communities despite living in a society that does not venerate eldership or make it easy to become an elder.

Valued or not, elders are still needed, perhaps more than ever. Industrial-strength overwork has hollowed out the day-to-day life of North American communities, leaving a great many people lonely and isolated. If we are to have any hope of re-creating a rich and vibrant community life in the future, we're going to need a whole lot more people with both the skills and the willingness to serve as elders.

It takes a long time and a great deal of practice to become an elder, perhaps even more so in a society that only reluctantly acknowledges that wisdom can come with age. If that's something you want for yourself, you'd best start early. (The next chapter may help you picture where you could play an elder role in your community.)

Two Sides of the Same Coin

Healthy self-worth is encapsulated in the phrase *I am lovable and capable*. And while lovability and capability are personal qualities, they are qualities that are primarily experienced through task and relationship. I experience my capability by being useful, by feeling like I matter, by demonstrating my competence in real tasks. I experience my lovability primarily in relationship with others.

Connection and purpose are the yin and yang of healthy self-worth. Our passions and purposes carry us out in the world and engage us in human connections. Loving and caring for family, friends, and community give us a sense of place and purpose in the world. Having looked at the purpose side of coin, it is time now to turn to its obverse: connection.

CHAPTER FOUR

Gather a Tribe

In lives dominated by work, friendship circles have often begun to shrink by the time a person reaches mid-life. The workplace may satisfy enough of your need for connection that other kinds of relationship atrophy. It is easy to forget the skills of friendship not required by the workplace, or to allow them to become rusty. Parallelling the need for new purpose we saw in the last chapter, our circles of connection may require some attention and renewal at mid-life. First, though, we need to understand why connection is both important and problematic.

The Stress of Social Isolation

When people from other cultures visit North America, most of them notice two things immediately. One is the incredible amount of physical wealth we have. The other is how lonely people are.

There is a connection between these two observations. Poverty offers abundant opportunities for human connection that wealth eliminates. Sharing food, tools, and entertainment creates regular requirements for contact. When the only way to enjoy music is to get together to make it, and the only way to see a film is with half the village, it's hard not to be in regular human contact. Many Third World households have three or four generations living under one roof, with grandparents, aunts, uncles, and cousins all within earshot.

In North America, not only do we live in separate nuclear families and get much of our entertainment at home, but with many homes having multiple TVs, radios, and stereos, even home entertainment can be a solitary pastime. The automobile rules our outdoor urban spaces, making them unfriendly to conviviality.

Mobility further undermines our social connections. In many poorer parts of the world, and even in parts of Europe, people stay in the same community their whole lives. The average North American moves about once every five years. Even if you stay put, it's likely your neighbours will not.

Urban life also increases anonymity. For me, living in a small town, it's hard to go to the grocery store or a movie or a public dance without running into someone I know. When you bump into the same people regularly, people become acquaintances and friends almost accidentally. In a big city, when you go out in public it usually means being surrounded by strangers.

The relentless intensification of work in North America means that even social contacts in the workplace are becoming increasingly brief and non-intimate. The combination of long workweeks and the "Second Shift" of domestic duties carried by dual-earner households means that many people have neither the time or the energy for friendship or community activities.

People seldom recognize what a huge stress the social isolation of North American life has become. The results of a large study in Alameda County, California, give an idea of its impact. Researchers interviewed thousands of men and women to determine the number and types of contacts each had with family, friends, and community groups. For the next seventeen years, researchers monitored the health and mortality of the people they had interviewed and found that those who had the fewest social connections were two and a half times more likely to die than those who had the strongest social ties. Subsequent studies in Georgia, Massachusetts, Connecticut, Iowa, Sweden, and Finland all found similar results. The increase in mortality caused by social isolation was right across the board: more heart disease, more cancer, more suicide, more accidental deaths, and more infectious disease deaths.[1]

Making Connection a Priority

There's a phrase we sometimes use in counselling: I can't fill your cup if you hold it upside down. As well as creating a great deal of social isolation, North American culture reinforces this isolation by placing an inordinately high value on independence. The Marlboro Man is a loner who needs no one. If you want relationships, some people might judge you as being "needy." Children are allowed to be needy, but adults are supposed to be "strong." In such a culture it's tempting to ease the hurt of loneliness by building a scar of denial over it. You deny fears of being hurt or rejected by pretending you are anti-social by nature.

Though some people clearly have a gift for the skills of connection, anyone can become better at friendship skills if they invest energy and attention into learning and practice. Before that can happen, however, you need to acknowledge your wish for intimacy and connection. You have to feel your longing and give it the attention it deserves.

Setting goals around relationship may be more important to your well-being than the financial goal-setting that so often pre-occupies people at mid-life. In his research on the high price of materialism, psychologist Tim Kasser discovered that meeting materialist goals — goals around money, possessions, and social status — resulted in disappointingly small and fleeting increases in the happiness levels reported by his study participants. In contrast, meeting non-materialist goals had a much larger and far more durable positive impact on participants' happiness. Those non-materialist goals often had to do with either people's relationships or their connection to their community. What Kasser's research suggests is that making connection a priority in your life has a much larger capacity to create fulfillment in your life than other, more materialistic goals.[2]

Circles of Relationship

A useful way to begin paying more attention to connection in your life is to review the current state of your relationships. I'd like to invite you to try an exercise I do with my heart health groups. Take a blank, unlined piece of paper. In the centre draw a circle about 2.5 inches in diameter. Around that circle draw a second circle about 5 inches in diameter.

In the inner circle write the names of anyone you see on a daily or almost daily basis. Include work contacts, neighbours, and family members. In between the inner circle and the outside circle write the names of people or groups you see once every week or so. If you routinely seek out specific individuals within those groups, list them separately. So, for instance, if you go out with the hiking club most weeks, and on most hikes you walk and talk with Rene and Chris, list Rene and Chris as well as the hiking club. Around the outside of the page list all the people and groups you see only occasionally.

When you're done, take a look at the pattern that has emerged. Which circle is most crowded? Least crowded? If you removed work relationships, how much would remain? Who initiates the contact between you and the people in your circles? How did the people in your circles come into your life? Who's new, and who's been around a long time? Who is farther out than you would like? Who is closer in than is comfortable? Are your circles as full as you would like? Are there particular kinds of relationships that are missing? What do you like about what you see? What do you wish was different?

Your proficiency with friendship skills is possibly even more important than the size of your friendship circle. Over time, friends move away or die or develop different interests. Without good skills to initiate, maintain, and enjoy friendships, your friendship circle will shrink. Take a few minutes now to do an inventory of your friendship skills. Reviewing your "Circles of Relationship" page may help get you started. Thinking about the following questions might also be useful.

✧ Where and how can you meet people who share your interests and passions?
✧ Where and how can you meet people who are different from you?
✧ How well can you engage a complete stranger in conversation?
✧ Do you know how to turn an acquaintance into a friend?
✧ How do you set boundaries when others are intrusive or untrustworthy? (This may not sound like a "friendship" skill, but if you don't have it, you'll be reluctant to invite new people into your life.)
✧ How do you nurture and maintain relationships with the people you care about?
✧ How do you handle conflict and anger?
✧ Are you able to be vulnerable?
✧ Can you receive as well as give?

Another way to explore your connectedness in the world is to review the different kinds of relationships in your life. In the sections that follow, it is useful to identify both strengths and gaps in your relationship life.

Family Connections

The diversity of family structures in North American society, and the wide range of ages at which people are choosing to have children — or not have children, or begin second families — mean that we might face quite different family issues at any given age. That being said, most of us have to deal with major changes in our relationships with family sometime early in the second half of life.

Parenting Your Parents

There is a reasonable likelihood that one or both of your parents will either suffer a health crisis or need some sort of regular assistance and support from you before you turn sixty-five. If you've been able to cut back to part-time work, it will be easier to find time to meet those needs without going crazy or burning out. Maybe your parents will stay in perfect health till a ripe old age, but it's one of those "jokers" in the deck of life that you should be prepared to face.

If life has estranged you from your parents, the longer you wait, the more likely it is they will die without that wound being healed. Often the reversal of roles, when we are taking care of them instead of them taking care of us, can shake us out of old ways of relating to each other. Sometimes just spending more time together achieves the same result. Sometimes the imminence of death pushes both sides to reach past whatever blocks there may have been in the past.

Establishing a New Relationship with Grown-Up Children

For parents — unless we had our children very early or very late — the years between forty-five and sixty-five are often when we must remake relationships with our children. While we might still want to provide advice, support, and material assistance to our grown children, it won't work to continue treating them like children. We need to respect their right to make their own lifestyle choices, even if they make choices we wouldn't make.

Grown children can benefit from a certain amount of parental guidance, but it must be given to a twenty-five-year-old with a much gentler, softer touch than we'd use for an eight-year-old. We need to learn what Gail Sheehy calls "skills of influence."[3]

Young adults have to find their own way in the world and to make their own mistakes on occasion. Saying "I told you so" may be good for your ego, but it does not help your adult offspring.

Grandparenthood

In most other societies around the world, grandparents serve as assistant parents. In a number of cultures, grandparents are the primary caregivers of the young. In North America, people choose whether and how much to be involved with grandchildren.

The skills of good grandparenting are different than the skills of good parenting. With luck, your experience of raising children has taught you some of the art of parenting. On the other hand, it is your sons or daughters and their partners who have primary responsibility for the care of your grandchildren. Your role shifts from quarterback to coach. You will want to pass on to your children what you can of the knowledge you learned as a parent. At the same time, if you undermine your child's parenting self-confidence, or undercut his or her rules, or get caught in a power struggle over how to parent, you are not helping your children *or* your grandchildren.

One of the gifts of grandparenthood is that it is often easier to unconditionally love our grandchildren than our children. It's hard not to see children as 3-D report cards on our skill as parents. It's also easy to "need" our children to succeed in some way we didn't. While a parent may have a prescription for who their child is supposed to be, a grandparent might have a more disinterested curiosity, wondering exactly who this person is who has been born into the family.

Extended Family/Extending Family

The closest thing we have in North America to a traditional clan or tribe is our extended families. Between busyness and mobility, maintaining relationships with our larger family can be difficult and time-consuming, but for many people, family members are the only people with whom we have relationships that are measured in decades rather than years.

Every year on the first Saturday in December, all my relatives on my paternal grandfather's side meet for a party at the same restaurant in Weston, Ontario. Living frugally at the opposite end of the country, I don't always get to the gathering. But I know each December it will happen, and I can catch up on the news of my various aunts, uncles, cousins, nieces, and nephews by checking in with those who did attend.

I know of other extended families who overcome the con-straints of geography by vacationing together or through a shared family interest such as sailing or Celtic music.

Some families are more porous than others and might be called "extending" families. If a marriage ends, ex-wives and stepchil-dren still remain part of the family. Close family friends and occasionally even neighbours may join the clan.

Adopting Family

I left Ontario and moved to BC as a young man before the days of e-mail. Long-distance phone calls were expensive enough that — in my family, at least — you didn't chat for long. I felt the loss of easy contact with my parents. As I passed through Argenta, BC, I stopped in to visit a Quaker couple I had met when they were facilitators at a study centre north of Toronto. John and Helen Stevenson were warm, curious, and welcoming people in their early sixties, good role models of Quaker values.

I arrived several months after a fire had destroyed the Steven-sons' home. For some technical reason I cannot remember, they had not been able to insure it adequately, so the insurance pay-ment they received was enough to cover only the cost of materi-als. John and Helen were rebuilding the house themselves, with volunteer help from a number of friends. I stuck around for almost a month, working for room and board, as a member of what we laughingly called the Nearly Adequate Construction Company, and I "adopted" John and Helen. When I moved to nearby Nelson, they helped me find my balance in a new place a long way from home and family.

I wasn't the only one to adopt John and Helen. Their eldest son, David, used to make tongue-in-cheek complaints that his parents had so many "adopted" children and grandchildren that he had to make appointments to see them. I remember the day a community work bee was organized to help with the rebuilding. It's amazing what two hundred people can get done in a day! The huge turnout was in part a reflection of Argenta's tight-knit community, but it was also evidence of the number of people who had special relationships with Helen and John. Wise hearts are a special gift.

Are you impatient for your children to have children so that you can have little people in your life again? Why wait? It's far easier to adopt a grandchild than to adopt a child. All it requires is that you reach out and open yourself to caring for a little person who isn't your own flesh and blood. There are volunteer grandparent programs in many schools. Daycare centres always need volunteers. Schools and recreation centres are perennially short of coaches for sports teams. Most single parents are seriously overloaded and would love to have someone to help out occasionally.

If you are single, widowed, or divorced, are you living alone because you want to live alone or because you don't have a partner? I often hear long-time singles in their fifties say, "I've lived alone so long, I'd have a hard time sharing my space with anyone else." That may be true, but there's a good deal of evidence that living alone isn't good for you either. Cooking for one isn't fun. People who live alone have markedly higher all-cause mortality rates than those who live with others, and it only gets worse as we get older. Shared living arrangements require energy, attention, and forbearance. In return they offer economy and conviviality.

In her book *Fountain of Age*, Betty Friedan describes how she, as a fifty-something divorcee, got together with several of her friends and rented a large house. Living together, eating together, the friends became family to one another. Many years after the co-op ended, the relationships formed in that house were still among Friedan's inner circle.[4]

Friendships

The second half of life can often involve serious changes in our friendship circle. How many of your friendships are tied to the workplace? How many would continue if you left your job or were laid off? How many of your friends come via shared parenting roles? How will those relationships change as your children leave home? If you have thoughts of moving somewhere warmer, or to a smaller town, once you've finished with your current job, how many friends do you have in that new place?

It is tempting, in the hurly-burly of modern life, to make your spouse your best and only friend, but this leaves you vulnerable if your spouse dies or if your relationship hits the skids. Friends can be our lifeline to sanity sometimes. Good friends also provide a sub-floor of emotional safety if the bottom falls out of your life without warning.

Let's imagine that tomorrow morning you become a modern-day Job. Your employer calls to say your job is being terminated immediately; it appears that someone has embezzled large amounts of money from your employer and done a good job setting you up as the fall guy. Your bank calls to say your account is overdrawn, and in the course of the conversation you discover that someone has emptied all your investment and banking accounts. The mortgage company calls to let you know that because of the police investigation and your job termination, it is calling due your house mortgage, effective immediately. Your spouse and children are nowhere to be found. You have no idea what happened to them, whether they have been kidnapped or are shunning you for reasons unknown.

Who would you go to for comfort? If you needed to be housed and fed for a week or a month, or if you were so messed up you felt unable to function, on whose doorstep would you park yourself? If that person couldn't help, for whatever reason, how many other friends do you trust would take you in if you showed up one day at their home as a complete basket case?

As you ponder your "Job list," don't beat yourself up if you feel chagrined by the answer. North American culture is good at creating social isolation. What's important to notice is that friends create a special kind of safety in the world.

Occasionally we meet people we click with so instantly that one or two contacts can quickly set us on the road to friendship. Much of the time, however, friendships happen in our life because we are involved in activities or networks that bring us into regular contact with new people, because we make time and space available for friendship, because we reach out to new people.

Food and friendship go well together. Churches and clubs that hold potluck gatherings seem to have a much greater ability to create bonds between members. Weekly supper clubs can be a powerful nurturer of friendships.

Some people turn their friends into a tribe by mixing and matching them wherever possible. Our friends may not always get along with each other, but when they do it can create a powerful synergy. I can remember, many years ago, living in a large co-op house where we all took turns inviting our friends to dinner. Over time "our friends" became one large circle, creating an incredible sense of richness I still remember with fondness.

Though the ability to make new friends is useful, the gift of hanging on to people from our past is also useful. As with many of the skills of friendship, women often seem better at it than men. The movies *Steel Magnolias* and *The Ya-ya Sisterhood* did a good job of conveying the power of deep-rooted relationships.

Like many of my gender, I have let myself lose touch with too many good people over the years. Working on this chapter has started to shift that for me.

I've known my first wife, Mary, for thirty years now. We actually did fairly well in choosing each other; we were just too inexperienced in relationships for our marriage to survive the learning curve. In the intervening years we've managed to become good friends. For many years, however, despite valuing our connection, we allowed it to be haphazard. She lived near my parents, so I would visit her whenever I went back east to see them. If I didn't get back home for a while, I wouldn't talk to Mary.

Over the last year or so we've taken to calling each other about once a month. She knows me well. Often when I talk with her I gain a clearer understanding of what's going on for me. Mary reports a similar benefit. There's an ease and familiarity that comes with knowing each other through so many changes. I don't know why we allowed our connection to be catch-as-catch-can for so long. Making it more consistent feels like being generous to ourselves where we had been stingy.

I've also come to realize that it is more important to recognize friendship than it is to understand it. My relationship with my friend Maggi is a case in point. We met at a conference almost twenty years ago. We liked each other immediately. There was also some physical attraction, but neither of us was single, so we just flirted. (Afterwards she sent me a card that said, "Thanks for the fantasy.") We shared a common professional interest in family-friendly work schedules, which occasionally brought us to the same conferences and gave us an excuse to keep sending resource materials back and forth. Always, though, our e-mails and phone conversations would drift back and forth between the personal and the professional. Eventually we began to call each other strictly to yak.

Years later, and Maggi is on my Job list. If I was destitute and in a bad way, I would feel perfectly comfortable throwing myself on her mercy. (She lives a thousand miles away, which would seem to keep her reasonably safe from that outcome, but I know that if either of us thought the other was really in trouble, we'd send the airfare.)

I've seen Maggi in person maybe half a dozen times. Our communication has been mostly through e-mail and telephone calls — neither of which are normally big favourites of mine. My strong preference for face-to-face contact is one reason I've tended to lose touch with friends when geography has separated us, yet my connection with Maggi formed on the very channels that strangled other relationships. For a long time it was Maggi who kept the relationship going. I've gotten better in recent years at holding up my end. Part of what's changed has been my recognition that our connection has not respected the limitations that circumstances should have placed upon it.

I'm sure many people believe in reincarnation because there are some relationships where we *recognize* the other person rather than having to gradually negotiate the passage between stranger and friend. I've been getting better at noticing when relationships make their own rules, and at giving them the space to do so.

Community Connections

For most of human history, people have lived in tribes or extended clans. The only time they lived alone was when their whole tribe had died or when the tribe had banished them for some major crime. I think we are genetically programmed to want to belong to a tribe, to want regular contact with other human beings. We no longer live, eat, and work in the same tribe. But any group of people that meets regularly, and where everyone knows everyone else, can function as a tribe.

Where do the important people in your life come from? Some come from the family tribe you were born into — what about the rest? Most of the time, the friends who have become important in our lives are people we have had the opportunity to hang out with again and again in one or other tribal gathering. If you feel a yen to "adopt" a child or grandchild, it's much easier if you belong to a tribe that spans the generations. You won't make those connections playing bridge at a senior's centre or living in an Adults Only complex where children are banned.

What tribes do you belong to now? What tribes have you belonged to in the past? Sometimes the only way to find our own tribe is to create it. Carolyn Shaffer and Kristin Anundsen's *Creating Community Anywhere* is an excellent how-to guide for finding and creating all kinds of communities, from co-housing to electronic communities to Twelve Step groups.[5]

With imagination, it is possible to create community even in environments that might seem hostile to it. For instance, I've always been a little leery of travelling in a motorhome, thinking I'd feel isolated and aimless after a while. But you don't have to give up the travelling life to find purpose and connection. About a thousand "Care-A-Vanners" now travel around the country in small convoys of RVs, building homes together as Habitat for Humanity volunteers.

Neighbourhood Tribes

Neighbourhoods can become tribes. Do you know your neighbours? If you needed to borrow a cup of sugar, how many of your neighbours would you feel comfortable asking? How many of your neighbours would feel comfortable asking you? If teenagers moved into a house in your neighbourhood and began throwing loud, drunken parties, what would happen? Would your neighbourhood be able to make some sort of collective response?

Sometimes we're lucky enough to live in a place that already has well-established neighbourhood links. Other times we need to be the catalyst if we want to create a neighbourhood tribe. All it requires is a few people willing to find excuses to get together: a block barbecue party, a tool-sharing co-op, neighbourhood fireworks, a Halloween party, or a carol sing. Perhaps you can set up a video collective that passes around seven-day videos or, better yet, watches them together. Or you could establish a Slow Food supper club, a Neighbourhood Watch network, a car co-op, a tag-team after-school child care, or a neighbourhood association.

Sometimes the enforced separateness of North American residential patterns (i.e., fenced backyards, busy streets separating blocks of houses) works against the growth of community. Land co-ops and housing co-ops often do more than reduce the price of land and housing for people who buy in to them. They can also be a way to create a strong neighbourhood relationship. Another variant is co-housing, in which dwellings are clustered around a communal space, including a community kitchen where members may eat together one or several times per week.

Play Communities

Play has a wonderful capacity to connect people. When we laugh together, when we have fun together, it often connects us to people of different ages with different political beliefs.

Some kinds of activities seem to be able to attract people of all ages. Here in Courtenay there is a Fiddle Club with members ranging from under seven to over seventy years of age. There is a summer youth theatre program that involves adults of all ages in support roles. The hiking club includes children, grandparents, and everyone in between.

What play communities do you belong to? What fun things have you done in the past? What have you always wanted to do? Whether you arrange to meet people to play Scrabble or badminton, to rock climb, or to play in a weekend rock band, they're all ways to connect by having fun.

Faith Communities

Communities that form around shared spiritual beliefs can be a powerful force of connection because they not only link us to our local community, but also plug us into a much wider faith network. Religious connections are among the most likely to continue for years and decades. Faith communities can unite us across age and social class boundaries. Many times they provide opportunities to join with others in acts of service.

Sometimes small study, prayer, or meditation groups attached to faith communities are better means of building relationships than weekly religious services, where interaction is limited.

Support Groups

Support groups often act as a form of family for people in times of crisis or grief. They can be a source of strength for people struggling with an addictive relationship to alcohol, drugs, food, gambling, or work. Support groups can provide fellowship and sustenance for those who want to break free of traditional gender roles or to live more frugally.

Cause Collectives and Service Tribes

Groups built around social causes or service to the community often give us a sense of purpose as we work towards shared goals, while allowing us to feel solidarity with others who share similar passions. Whether the cause is global in scope — world peace, for example — or local — setting up a neighbourhood Montessori School — it connects us with other people. Service clubs typically combine networking and socializing with an intent to find concrete ways to help out in the local community.

Building a Good Foundation

It's easy in North America to wind up as a senior spending most of your days alone in front of the TV, which is often the pain-reliever of choice for lonely people. And because you rarely make friends sitting in front of the TV, while TV eases the pain of isolation, it also prolongs it. However, despite the personal and social pressures I have outlined, loneliness and isolation are not necessary outcomes of growing older. In fact, when you look at who in North America has the richest and most satisfying social networks, seniors are disproportionately *over-represented*.

The importance of relationships to your health and happiness later in life is a central theme of all the successful aging literature. Robert Kahn and John Rowe declare, "The bottom line is, we do not outgrow our need for others. The life-giving effect of close social relations holds throughout the life course."[6]

David Snowdon hypothesizes that the communal life of the nuns he studied was one reason they outlived average American women. Within his study group, a richness in social relationships was associated with being happier, healthier, and longer lived. Snowdon reported that a particularly vital and ebullient ninety-year-old, when asked why she was always so "up," replied, "Maybe it's because I've always been with the young."[7]

George Vaillant was also struck by the fact that those who showed the most vitality in the second half of life were well connected to others. He gives the example of Susan Wellcome, who at age seventy-six still edited a newsletter for the World Council of Churches and regularly invited teenagers into her working-class Akron home to play pool.[8]

What else do the successful aging researchers tell us? All of them agree that all-at-once retirement can be traumatic, particularly for men, and particularly for those who retire and move at the same time. (We will talk more about both potential pitfalls in Chapters Six and Seven.)

Another common theme is that the happiest and healthiest seniors have friends of all ages. If your friends span the age spectrum, it's easy to stay in touch with the continuity of life. If your friendship circle is limited to your contemporaries, they will eventually start to get frail and senile and die, and your worldview will be one of deterioration and loss.

As an older acquaintance of mine once remarked, "The advantage of having much younger friends is that you so rarely have to go to their funerals." If your friendships take you to weddings and graduations and christenings more often than to funerals, it's a constant reminder that the web of life continues.

Diversity should include more than age. Too often retirement becomes a retreat from the world because people avoid the challenge of connecting with people different from themselves. The happiest of seniors seem to welcome this challenge. They seek out people who are different and enjoy having friends of different ages, from different cultures, with different opinions. As one such person said to me, only partly in jest, "How can you have a good argument with someone who thinks the same way you do?"

One final conclusion of all the successful aging researchers is that a rich circle of connection later in life doesn't happen by accident. Seniors who had rich social connections made relationship a high priority in their lives, and most had done so for a long time. There's no better way to insure that you'll end up a happy, well-connected senior than to create a richness of relationship for yourself when you're fifty.

The Heart of the Matter

When you read the literature on human happiness, what is striking is that having more money has almost no measurable impact on how happy people report themselves to be. Relationships, on the other hand — marriage, family, friendship, and community connections — are crucial to people's happiness.

Your relationships will likely have more impact on your future happiness than your salary. You will probably create more love and joy in the world through your relationships than through anything you do for money. Are these simple truths reflected in how you live? How much time and energy do you make available for the important people in your life? Do you live as though your relationships are your top priority? If not, you have an opportunity to change in the second half of life.

CHAPTER FIVE

Get Bigger and Wilder

The final step to claiming your freedom is learning to see the second half of life not as the loss of youth, but as the full flowering of all you can be in the world — a coming to fruition.

If I am fearful of getting older, I will hold back and will not let myself go for the adventure of the second half. If I unthinkingly accept our society's ageist prejudices, I will limit my freedom without even knowing I am doing so. I will fail to see the new pleasures, new challenges, and new opportunities that are available to me.

In this chapter I first want to look at our need for challenge. I will show how addressing that need has the power to make the later years of your life turn out more like your hopes than your fears. Then I want to explore the second half of life as a new stage of growth and becoming by looking at six of the most important tasks of character development.

The Fundamental Choice

I'd like to begin with the fundamental choice each of us faces in the second half of life: Are you going to get bigger or are you going to get smaller?

Think about the seniors you know or have known. Who got

smaller? I can think of people who retired to gated seniors' communities. First they became afraid to leave those communities, then afraid to leave their units, and finally fearful that even the staff who came in to clean would rob them.

Physically they became smaller, with a smaller and smaller range of motion. They didn't make new friends. As old friends died, their circle of connection shrank. They became less curious. They didn't learn new skills. Their brains got slow and rusty from lack of use.

Some people shrank by becoming more and more innocuous. Their response to anything was "Whatever you say, dear" or "I'm just an old lady — what does it matter what I think?" Others got smaller by becoming rigid and judgmental.

Getting smaller is the default program for seniors in our society. It's what will happen to you if you're not paying attention, if you fail to choose something different. Our society makes it easy for older people to retreat from life.

Now let's look at the other choice. Who do you know who got bigger with the passage of time? Who became more themselves, more *real*, the older they got? There's an interesting paradox when I ask myself that question, because the number of people I can think of who got bigger is smaller than the number who got smaller, but the people who got bigger occupy more room in my heart. They feel almost larger than life.

Ruth Masters is one of my personal examples of a person who keeps getting bigger. At eighty-three she still hikes and does trail work in the mountains, even though her knees are giving her grief. She knows there are risks to being there, but she says, "There's no place I'd rather die than up a mountain somewhere."

Ruth is an active environmentalist, fundraising to preserve special pieces of land. She's no stranger to non-violent civil disobedience in defence of the environment. "It's great being old," she says with a twinkle in her eye, "because they don't know what to do with you."

As well as making signs in her basement for local hiking trails,

Ruth creates engraved, stainless steel spoons for anyone she knows or hears about who has done something good or important for the community. Receiving a "Hero" spoon from Ruth is an important honour.

Ruth is always out and about at public events. She is opinionated, certainly, but also curious and open. There's a playfulness about her. She's one of those people everyone seems to know, and when her name is mentioned, people smile.

In this chapter I want to address the question, What is it that makes some people get bigger, while others shrink with the passage of time?

The Three Circles of Life

Many people see retirement as a kind of safe harbour. They have no responsibilities; they no longer have to take risks; they can take it easy and coast. If you relate to the second half of life that way, you will shrink, I guarantee it.

Why? Imagine that your life is made up of three circles. In the inner circle are activities that are completely familiar and predictable to you. The inner circle is a comforting place to visit. As a place to live, it's boring.

Around the outer perimeter of your life are all those activities so completely unknown and unpredictable that they are terrifying. It's not a fun place, even for a short visit.

In between the circle of the completely known and the completely unknown is the circle of adventure, filled with activities that are somewhat familiar, but with sufficient newness and unpredictability to offer challenge.

Life tends to be most satisfying when we spend enough time in the inner circle to feel secure, and enough time in the middle circle to feel a sense of challenge and excitement.

An unfortunate fact about the three circles is that they are not static. If you spend your days in the inner circle, the outer circle will steadily push inwards till it starts to nibble away at the inner circle. In fact, there seems to be some either/or function: If you're not actively making that middle circle bigger, the outer one creeps in on you.

If your idea of retirement is that you're always going to feel safe and comfortable, your life will be boring. You will be boring. And you will shrink.

If you want the second half of your life to feel like an adventure, if you want to feel excited and fully alive, you'll need to challenge yourself, push the edges, do things you've never done before. You need to set up new opportunities for yourself to learn and grow — when you're fifty, and even when you're ninety. That's the price you pay if you want to keep getting bigger as you get older.

In talking about the choice to get bigger or smaller, I am not talking about something hypothetical or future tense. If work has been dominating too much of your life for too long, by mid-life you're probably already starting to shrink. Your circle of friendships may be getting smaller. You may be less involved in your community. Your range of interests and hobbies may be shrinking. Being overweight or unfit may already be limiting your physical capabilities. Theoretically, all those losses can be reversed when you retire, but the smaller you get, the harder it's going to be to turn the tide. The best way to ensure that you'll get bigger rather than smaller in the second half of life is to start getting bigger right now.

Six Challenges for the Second Half of Life

Perhaps the most pernicious of the common ageist ideas in our society is the assumption that because old people's bodies show some wear and deterioration, no more growth is possible for them. While it's true that some older people do choose to stop growing, it is neither necessary nor healthy to do so.

People who write about the second half of life consistently name six character traits demonstrated by Successful Agers: openness, outrageousness, self-possession, wisdom, soulfulness, and resilience. As you enter the second half of your life, seize the opportunity for growth and development — take up the challenge of developing these traits in yourself.

Openness

I met Lila Carrol when I was twenty-six. She was eighty-two. I had travelled across Canada in a Volvo station wagon, which I had outfitted as a camper. Lila was a relative of a friend of a friend. The friend had said, "If you get as far as Courtenay, call Lila — you'll really like her." I did call Lila, not even quite sure why. "Yes," she said, "come for tea." I went for tea, and Lila immediately began asking questions. She asked questions more personal than I would usually expect to be asked by a complete stranger. She also told me about herself and invited my questions. She invited me to stay in her spare room for a day or two. Over the next two days we talked and talked. By the time I left I felt I knew Lila better than many people I had known for years. She already knew more about me than most people did. Sometimes I suspect I eventually moved to Courtenay in part because of how welcome Lila made me feel.

What was it about Lila that made our contact so powerful?

Her door was open. I may have been the one who took the first step by calling her, but in a very real way Lila was the one who initiated the relationship. She invited me to her home. Once I was there, she invited me to stay. She invited me to tell her about myself. She looked for ways she could connect to me rather than fearing me as a stranger. She wasn't without caution — she invited me to tea and looked me over before inviting me to stay — but she took risks.

Lila was curious, curious about what my dreams were, curious about what I'd learned on my journey. She wanted to know what was important to me, what brought me joy, what caused me distress. She had strong religious beliefs, but they weren't etched in stone. "The truth isn't fragile," she said. Lila wanted to know what Quakerism was and how it was different. Her curiosity engaged us and opened me.

Lila was open-hearted. More than once she cried during those two days. She laughed a lot. She allowed me to see the places where she felt vulnerable, unsure, and sad. She allowed me to affect her. She was generous with her time and attention. She was willing to trust in my goodwill. She was fully present, fully herself.

I was twenty-six. I didn't usually hang out with "old ladies," with the exception of my maternal grandmother. But Lila was so Lila it was impossible to think of her as an old lady. When she talked about something that happened when she was twenty-two, the twenty-two-year-old was there in the room. When she talked about being seven, I encountered the seven-year-old.

Who have you known in your life who has shown an outsized ability to establish connection and print themselves large upon your soul? When we meet people who feel larger than life, it's easy to think they've always been that way, to forget that what we see is often the result of decades of practising the skills of open heart, open mind, open door.

Learning to be good at these skills requires that we make them a priority. The Buddha is reported to have said, "In the end, these things matter most: How well did you love? How fully did you live? How deeply did you learn to let go?"

Outrageousness

There is a liberation that can happen when we finally let go of needing to please or impress other people.

There are two important reasons why it serves you to learn to be outrageous in the second half of life. The first is that the roles our society prescribes for seniors are suffocatingly narrow. Seniors are supposed to relax somewhere in a hammock, play golf, perhaps go to a prayer meeting or two. They're not supposed to be too loud, too angry, too sexual, or too political. And they definitely shouldn't be living in communes.

Those old scripts for senior citizens are gradually breaking down as millions of seniors studiously ignore them. Nonetheless, it's good to cultivate a certain degree of chutzpah if you plan to get bigger as you get older.

The second reason why it's good to have outrageousness skills is that you may feel called to explore your shadow in the second half of life. Exploring the shadow means going into an area where you felt clumsy, inept, or embarrassed in the past. You need a particular kind of damn-the-torpedoes courage to explore the shadow.

Jane Juska is a wonderful example. Jane was a retired schoolteacher. Divorced and living alone, she had convinced herself for years that she was past being interested in sex. At age sixty-six she realized, No, it's not true. I *am* still interested. She placed the following ad in the "personals" column of the *New York Review of Books:*

Before I turn 67 — next March — I would like to have lots of sex with a man I like. If you want to talk first, Trollope works for me.[1]

Over the next year, Juska had romantic and erotic relationships with several men, including one half her age. (She even found a man who shared her appreciation for novelist Anthony Trollope.) Then she described the whole experience in a book — *A Round-Heeled Woman* — that became a bestseller. That's how outrageous you can be if you don't let others decide what you can or cannot do in the second half of life.

Sam Keen was a successful writer and teacher of philosophy. One month before his sixty-second birthday he went to his first class at Trapeze School. That's right, trapeze as in the circus, as in flying trapeze. He became hooked immediately, eventually set-ting up a trapeze in his backyard so that classes could be held there. In his mid-sixties, he and his friends established a "fly-ing" school called Upward Bound.[2]

Juska and Keen both offer us examples, not just of how to be outrageous in the second half of life, but also of where that chal-lenge often lies. It's hard enough to be outrageous in an arena where we feel talented and experienced. In the second half of life we are often challenged to go where we feel least capable and most unsure of ourselves.

Juska's book shows that she was clearly a gifted and experi-enced teacher. It would have been relatively comfortable for her to push the boundaries of teaching or teacher training. It was easy for Juska to be successful at teaching, to be praised for her teaching. It was so easy, in fact, that for many years she had used an obsession with teaching to push down and push aside her longing for intimacy. Teaching wasn't where Jane felt lacking or incomplete in her life. Relationships, particularly sexual rela-tionships, was an area where she was woefully inexperienced and lacking in confidence. To feel whole and complete, at age sixty-six she had to go back and do what she had been too afraid and too wounded to do as a younger woman.

Sam Keen also had to leave his strengths behind to go where his dreams demanded. He'd spent his life as a philosopher, living in the kingdoms of the mind. What connection he'd had with his body had been macho — strong, hard, in charge. To excel on the trapeze he had to learn grace and softness, had to learn a new kind of trust in his body. But again, there was no academic suc-cess he could imagine that had the immediate excitement of "learning to fly."

It is a natural human tendency to do what we're good at, to focus our energies where they are rewarded, and to avoid activi-ties where we feel clumsy, inadequate, or unsure of ourselves.

Maybe in the first half of your life you developed a strong, sharp mind. Perhaps you've become so good at thinking that you use your mind to solve every problem, even the problems where a soft heart is needed. To enter the world of the soft heart, you'll need to leave all that expertise behind. You'll need to become a rank amateur. You'll need to make dumb and embarrassing mistakes. And it's probably exactly what you need to do if you are ever to feel whole and complete in this life.

Entering into the shadow is not easy. Usually it requires us to go through the experiences we weren't willing to face when we were younger, with the added hitch that at age fifty or sixty we may have to learn skills others mastered in their teens.

Juska threw herself with abandon into learning about men and sex. Her interest, excitement, and pleasure were, if anything, heightened by decades of avoidance and delay. The fact that she was on the steep end of her learning curve was just how it was. Pleasure and pain were intermixed on this journey.

Sam Keen is quick to admit that, after several years and thousands of hours learning trapeze, he is still limited in his skills. It doesn't matter. He finds immense joy in the learning. The physical metaphor of the trapeze has taught him a great deal about grace, surrender, trust, and courage.

As a teenager, I was always physically klutzy. When people were picked for sports teams, my younger brother would be chosen first. I would be last. Clumsy or not, I loved to dance. The 1960s, with their flail-about and let-it-all-hang-loose dance style, were a godsend to me. But what fascinated me was ballroom dancing — cha-cha, tango, jive — all that stuff where you and a partner have to move together. (To this day, *Dirty Dancing* and *Strictly Ballroom* are two of my all-time favourite movies.)

For many years the knowledge that I would be slow to learn, that I would probably never be really good, that I would always have periodic freeze-ups where my feet refused to move, was enough to inhibit me from taking dance classes. At fifty-two I don't care. I'm doing it anyway. And while I often still feel clumsy, I also feel new and excited. While ballroom dancing doesn't raise eyebrows the way being a sexy or airborne senior citizen would, it remains a challenge for me to do a thing I ran away from for so long.

Self-Possession

In *The Force of Character*, Jungian psychologist James Hillman argues that our principal task in the second half of life is to become fully and unapologetically ourselves, to become "joyfully eccentric." The lines on our faces and the grey in our hair, Hillman would argue, are badges of character we should wear with pride.[3]

"Self-possessed" is the term we use to describe people who are relaxed and confident in their own skins. Self-possessed individuals have a certain strength and potency. They are more able to keep to their own course in life, whatever happens. They also have a capacity to give others space: If I don't need you to like me, if I don't need you to agree with me, if I don't need you to do things my way, I am more able to let you be yourself.

One of the keys to self-possession is owning all of who you are. Owning what you want even if what you want goes against your talents. Owning who you are even if society, your parents, or your children don't approve.

Self-possession can be learned. By paying attention to when and how you give away your sense of worth, you can learn to give it away less often. Adversity has its own opportunities in this regard. Losing a job or taking a politically unpopular stand can initially shake your sense of worth, but it becomes an ideal opportunity to learn to separate your worth from your social position.

One of the opportunities in the second half of life is to learn the inward half of the art of being happy. It is easy in the first half of life to seek happiness by accomplishing one or more outer goals.

You can put large amounts of time and effort into manipulating the exterior world.

In the second half of life, you can begin to see how much of your happiness — or misery — depends on what goes on between your ears.

There's an old Buddhist story about a young prince who loved the feel of carpet on his feet. He began carpeting his palace, then the palace grounds, and finally even the road to town. The cost of miles and miles of carpet was bankrupting his kingdom. Finally, in desperation, one of his ministers had special carpet-lined sandals made. The prince loved the sandals because now he walked on carpet everywhere he went.

It is easy for young people to think that things outside themselves will make them happy or satisfied. In the second half of life we are likely to notice how much more important than what happens to us is what we tell ourselves about what happens. Equally important to our pleasure is the ability to clear the mind of all the distractions and anxieties that prevent us from savouring the immediate moment. There's huge value to be had in learning to wear the prince's sandals.

Wisdom

Social scientists tell us that, as far as they are able to measure wisdom, older human beings are collectively no wiser than younger human beings. I don't think this means that it is arrogance or wishful thinking to aspire to become wise as you grow older. Rather, it indicates that for every older person who achieves wisdom as he or she ages, there is another old person who has retreated from life and who became less wise with the passage of time.

I can think of several people I know who were wiser at age twenty-five than they came to be at fifty-five or seventy-five. Fear and shrinkage do a good job of dumbing people down. I have also known people who kept learning and growing all through life, and the wiser they got, the more valuable they became to everyone who knew them.

The paradox of wisdom is that while wisdom is a destination worth seeking, don't imagine that you can ever arrive. All the wise people I have known had a striking humility about them. Know-it-alls make themselves impervious to learning; stagnation is the inevitable result. I am reminded of the old Zen koan which says that in a conversation between a wise man and a fool, the wise man will always learn more than the fool.

Soulfulness

Most North Americans, if asked, will say they believe human beings have a soul that survives the death of the body. But we don't spend a lot of time thinking about what that soul is and how it might differ from the ego.

The part of you that desperately needs to win at sports, is that your soul? How about the part that gets upset over sagging muscles? Perhaps not? Then where is your soul?

Ram Dass reports that the experience of growing older is very different in India than in North America. In India, the belief that the soul lives on through a multitude of lifetimes is a fundamental assumption, part of the everyday fabric of life. People carry their bodies, their gender, their egos, their life stories like a set of clothes that is worn today and discarded tomorrow. There is a conscious effort to experience life as a soul tied to God, rather than as an ego or a personality. Ram Dass observes further:

> Metaphysical awareness helps . . . by reducing the stress of our twin nemeses: the compulsion to "have it all" now, and the desperate clinging to things of the past, including our youth. Emphasis is placed on eternal matters, which relieves the suffering of fighting against nature. And because the goal is God, rather than thin thighs, fabulous pensions, and geriatric erections, the old in India enjoy a peace, after the storm of youth, which is largely unknown to aging Americans.[4]

We all die, sooner or later. Believing I have a soul that will survive death does not free me from the terror of dying if the "I" I feel myself to be is the husk left to rot after the seed is gone. If I am a body, a life story, and an ego, death will feel like the loss of everything. All the marker points of growing older will be scary to me because each brings me one step closer to death and dissolution.

So how does a person learn to experience the soul? Most writers on the subject ask us to notice when we feel ourselves outside of time, however briefly, and to seek out those moments. We may feel it when we talk to loved ones long dead. Ram Dass found it as a companion to people who were dying. Some people feel it in silence, in nature, in prayer. Others feel it when they surrender to loving. Sometimes soul emerges in particular moments: when we are holding a baby, walking quietly with a dear friend, sitting alone in the afternoon sun.

In the second half of life we all have the opportunity to untangle ourselves from the world's brouhaha and live with soulfulness. Soulfulness has a power to take us outside of time and to bond us to others in ways that transcend time.

For those strict materialists who believe that death is the end, full stop, the Buddhist sage Gelek Rinpoche reminds us that the universe is made up of three constituents: matter, energy, and consciousness. The first two may change form, but they cannot be destroyed. Why should consciousness be different?[5]

Death is a mystery. Maybe you don't believe we humans have souls. On the other hand, if one day you die and find you have one, it might be convenient if you are not a stranger to it.

Resilience

One of the attitudes most strongly associated with resilience in the second half of life is a willingness to accept and embrace change. If you want to become shrink-resistant as you get older, it's useful to learn what George Vaillant calls "mature defenses": "In everyday life, the term *mature defenses* refers to our capacity to turn lemons into lemonade and not to turn molehills into mountains" (italics in original).[6]

Vaillant reports that he had to learn to use only objective criteria when assessing the health of his study participants. To illustrate why, he describes meeting two study participants for their annual reviews. One identified himself as a "heart patient" and was anxious and withdrawn, afraid to exercise or be sexual. The second remembered halfway through his review, "Oh yeah, George, I had a small heart attack last year, so I'm paying more attention to getting enough exercise now." Vaillant found himself thinking one man was really sick, while the other was still healthy — till he reviewed their medical charts and found they had nearly identical heart conditions.

Mature defenses are not denial. Where the "heart patient" retreated, the man who had a "small" heart attack was actively engaged in improving his heart health. Where one person saw the heart attack just as something that had happened to him, the other adopted the *identity* of "heart patient."

I can remember years ago, as part of my education for working with handicapped individuals, receiving training about multiple sclerosis from Tim, a forty-something man with MS. Tim knew a whole lot about MS, but what impressed me most was his attitude. Where many people with MS got depressed or railed against the unfairness of it, Tim's attitude was simply "This is the hand I've been dealt, and my job is to play my hand the best way I know how."

He learned everything he could about MS and then measured what he had learned against his own experience. He noticed heat made his MS worse, so he changed his summer work schedule to avoid going out in the heat of the day. He experimented with dietary changes. He noticed that when he allowed himself to get tired, it aggravated his MS, so he paid particular attention to pacing himself. He noticed that whenever he got depressed, his MS got worse. His attitude became "Other people can afford to be depressed — I can't." He noticed that many people — especially children — related to a person in a wheelchair as a "crip-ple," but did not see a person on a motorized scooter that way, so he got himself a scooter.

One of the reasons MS is such a difficult illness is that while it generally causes progressive deterioration, it is also incredibly quixotic, getting worse or going into remission pretty much at random. Sometimes what Tim called his "bag of tricks" wouldn't work, and when they did work he could never be sure it wasn't just luck. Even that uncertainty, Tim would say, was part of the hand he'd been given to play.

Tim wasn't able to cure his MS, but for several years his symptoms diminished to the point that he was able to get his scooter in and out of his car by himself, and could drive using hand controls. He was thus able to stay mobile and retain the independence that comes with mobility. Perhaps more important, he was able to use his illness as a discipline to become a relentlessly positive person.

At its best, making lemonade from life's lemons goes beyond minimizing losses. It involves learning from whatever happens and finding the positive good in every situation.

At age sixty-five, Ram Dass had a massive stroke that nearly killed him. After months of pain it left him unable to walk and able to talk only slowly, with some aphasia. Initially he went through all the fear, anger, self-pity, and grief you might expect, but he was unwilling to be a "victim" of his stroke. Two years later, writing in *Still Here,* he talks about his stroke as both a gift and a teacher in his life. His stroke helped him slow down from an obsessive busyness. He tells how his difficulties speaking clearly and remembering words taught him the poetry and clarity that can come when few words replace many. He shares how his disability has helped him learn to receive, to be given to, rather than always needing to be the helper.

The longer we live, the more likely we are eventually to face change, infirmity, or loss associated with the passage of time. One of the central themes that emerges from Abigail Trafford's book

My Time is that, for most people, the second half of life involves large and often unexpected changes. "Jolts," she calls them.[7]

Trafford's book introduces us to dozens of individuals who are negotiating the mid-life years. Virtually every one of them has experienced one or several "jolts." Sometimes it's a health crisis, or at least a health scare. Sometimes it's the death of a parent. Harder still is the death of a son or daughter. And perhaps cruellest of all, just when a couple makes it over the finish line to retirement, one of them dies.

Marriages founder. Couples who have been "Mom" and "Dad" for years don't always succeed in finding new ways to be together once the kids have gone. Trafford herself became divorced a few years before she wrote her book.

Jobs disappear, sometimes without warning. The stock market can make mincemeat of a couple's retirement plans or, worse yet, their retirement income.

At fifty-two, I've already been through my first "jolt." Soon after I started work on this book, an eleven-year relationship unravelled. As often happens when a couple splits, the house where I had lived ceased to be my home. There were dislocations in my friendship circle. I went from being free of the need to work for money to not quite free.

When big and unexpected changes happen, we often perceive them initially as disasters. In the fullness of time, they may turn out to be blessings in disguise. Trafford repeatedly describes situations where one or other "jolt" was exactly the spur people needed to get on with life, to do that thing they really felt called to do. As well, almost without exception, the "jolts" included new opportunities and positive challenges, at least for those who were open to seeing them.

My own experience has been that along with the grief and loss and the sense of life being turned upside down, my "jolt" taught me a lot about the difference between need and want. Eighteen months later I am enjoying a new life and a delightful new still-not-sure-exactly-what-this-is-yet relationship.

Have you heard the story about the atheist mountain climber? He's near the top of a high mountain when a small avalanche sweeps him towards a cliff edge. At the last possible moment he manages to catch hold of a small shrub. He's hanging by one hand, with thousands of feet of empty space below him, unable to lift himself back up to the ledge above. The shrub he's holding is starting to work its way loose. Desperate and alone, he decides to pray. "Dear God," he says. "If you exist and you're listening, please tell me what to do." As the words leave his mouth, he feels the presence of something tremendously warm and powerful. A strong but gentle voice speaks to him. "Let go," it says. Terrified, he grabs hold of the bush more tightly and shouts back, "Like hell I will!"

Is your life a possession or a gift? Some people seem to relate to their lives as a series of earned rewards or entitlements: It's *my* job, *my* money, *my* spouse, *my* body, *my* life, and I'm going to hang on tight to what is *mine*.

Other people, particularly as they get older, come to see life as a gift. It's a gift of unknown duration; a gift that keeps changing in shape. When change happens they let go of the old — with sadness perhaps, but also with gratitude for the gift that has been given. And then they turn and ask, What gift is being offered to me now?

A 'Bigger' Commitment

The second half of life can be — often is — the best half. But it's not for wimps or sleepwalkers.

Courage is easier said than done. Recognizing the need to keep challenging yourself, however, can strengthen your resolve. If you want the second half of life to feel like an adventure, the starting place is to make a commitment to live courageously, a commitment to live on life's green and growing edge.

CHAPTER SIX

Handle Money with Simplicity

Over the last three chapters you have explored and envisioned what freedom in the second half of life might look like and feel like for you. You may have discovered freedom in areas of your life where you haven't been using it. This is where you can begin moving into a new life right away. You probably also found areas of your life where you feel blocked from doing what you'd really like to do. The next stage in the process is to clear away impediments to your freedom. For most people, those impediments can be summarized in two words: money and time. Let's start with money.

The prescription that North American society offers us for achieving freedom is to earn big pots of money. Get rich and then "you won't have to work no more." The trouble is, not many people seem to find freedom along that path. Time and again they fall victim to the axiom that expenses will rise until they meet or exceed income. For most people it's like trying to fill a bucket with a hole in it.

What if the key to happiness is not "more," but "enough"? Joe Dominguez and Vicki Robin, the best-selling authors of *Your Money or Your Life*, argue that the relationship between money and happiness is not a diagonal straight line that leads forever skyward, but rather an inverted parabola.

At first, when money is paying for basic necessities like food and shelter, a small increase in income brings a large increase in fulfillment. Then, as we move into comforts, expenditures bring smaller but still significant increases in happiness. Even the occasional luxury can add to our happiness.

At some point, though, as the amount of free time and energy we have diminishes, each new luxury purchase starts to eat away at our ability to enjoy what we have. The toys become clutter. The things that can best create ongoing happiness in life — friends, family, and community — get squeezed out by the pressure of paying for and caring for all our "stuff." We find ourselves too tired, too busy, and too stressed to enjoy what we have. Once we move beyond that high point of "enough," "more" can only make life more stressful and less fulfilling.

Dominguez and Robin argue that the unreasoning faith that more will make us happy has pushed most North Americans into the clutter zone. Furthermore, they suggest that most of us do the major portion of our spending on automatic pilot, and that much spending is addictive in that large amounts of time and energy are traded for a short-term "buyer's high."

What If Less Were More?

What if you could feel happier than you do now while spending far less? If you needed less money to be happy, you'd have a lot more options. You could earn what you needed working part-time or part-year. You'd have the option of working at a job you really loved, even if it didn't pay as much.

In recent years, millions of people across North America have been embracing intentional frugality as their path to freedom. *Voluntary simplicity* is the name usually given to this philosophy and the burgeoning movement it has spawned.

Our culture has such a love-hate relationship with money that many people think they "should" be happier living on less, and perhaps, if they were better people, they wouldn't need so much. They imagine that they could save money by living in a puritan, self-denying way. That's not what voluntary simplicity is about. It is about the possibility that you could feel more joy, contentment, satisfaction, and happiness in your life while spending less money — perhaps far less money — than you are now.

For many people, voluntary simplicity is the key that unlocks the overspent door, which in turn enables them to escape from the prison of industrial-strength overwork. However, voluntary simplicity also has great value in and of itself, even if your circumstances are such that you can put work in its place without changing your relationship to money. Voluntary simplicity involves claiming your freedom from those who would otherwise pull your strings.

There are thousands of advertisers and advertising psychologists who would like nothing better than to convince you every day to spend money you don't have to buy things you don't need to impress people you don't like. And when they're really good at what they do, you'll be absolutely convinced that it was all your idea.

Hundreds of times a day you're brainwashed by the best in the business. Advertisers have even worked out the ideal setting for effective hypnosis: when you're exhausted after work, zoned out in front of the TV.

Juliet Schor reports in *The Overspent American* that when employees of a large telephone company were polled, a clear inverse relationship between saving habits and TV watching emerged. For each hour of television respondents watched, their personal savings would fall by an average of $4. That's how good at manipulation the advertisers are. To know how often they've been in your head, you only have to look in your wallet.

In a society like ours, with so many advertisers pulling at your strings, if you're not conscious about money — if you make purchases on automatic pilot — you can be sure that much of what you spend has more to do with their goals than yours. If you're not in command of your own strings, someone else is pulling them for you.

In this chapter I'll suggest several strategies for transforming your relationship with money. Collectively, they have the power to leave you feeling freer and more in charge of money in your life.

Epicurus's Question

The Greek philosopher Epicurus lived in the third century BC and had a fondness for good food and fine wine. His name lives on in the modern term for someone who loves fine dining, "epicure." Epicurus also laid out the first explicit rationale for voluntary simplicity.

Epicurus argued that human beings need only three things to be happy: friends, freedom, and an analyzed life. By friends he meant all our bonds of affiliation — friends, family, and community. By freedom he meant what we would call free time or leisure. By an analyzed life he meant that people need to understand not just what makes them happy, but what makes them happy in enduring ways.

Epicurus's observation was that many sources of happiness are transitory. They are intense but last a short time. The economics of happiness was simple for Epicurus. If people had to go through large amounts of pain and effort for a brief thrill of pleasure, the net impact on their happiness was negative. Only when people put their energy into enduring sources of happiness did the payoff of ongoing good feelings exceed the necessary investment of time and effort.

The pleasures that Epicurus identified as transient, modern psychologists would label as ego satisfactions. They include seeking after wealth, power, and social status or winning in one or other contest. The pleasures Epicurus identified as long-lasting were what we normally would think of as heart pleasures: love, friendship, and service. For Epicurus, the way to maximize happiness was to minimize the energy you put into transient ego "highs" so as to leave more time and energy available for the durable pleasures of the heart. Two thousand years later it's still good advice.

What provides lasting satisfaction in your life? One thing I have noticed is that the richest and most enduring pleasures in life are often shared. Life's enduring satisfactions tend to erase the distinction between selfish and unselfish. The pleasure that comes when you can lift a friend from distress and make him or her laugh — is that selfish or unselfish? The delight you feel when you help a child learn to ride a bicycle for the first time is a sweet pleasure precisely because it is shared.

Even with physical possessions it is important to notice when satisfaction runs counter to cost. For a few years I owned both a powerboat and a kayak. The powerboat cost a lot more to buy than the kayak. It cost more to run. It cost more to maintain. Yet when I searched my memory for pleasant boating experiences, most of them involved the kayak. Needless to say, the powerboat is now history.

Each month when I review my finances I ask myself, What felt good this month and cost nothing? One of the ironies of modern life is that many of the activities most capable of gladdening our hearts are free and easily available, but they get pushed aside by the pressure of paying for and maintaining a plethora of possessions that have much less ability to generate lasting satisfaction. When you cut back on addictive consumerism, it usually frees up both time and energy for the simple, enduring pleasures of life.

Sometimes less really is more. If your life is overstuffed with things and activities, simply getting rid of low-fulfillment expenditures will bring a positive improvement to your life. Clutter creates stress. Hurry creates stress. As we saw in Chapter

Two, stress sabotages your ability to enjoy what you have. I have noticed that when I try to stuff too many activities in a day — even if they're all fun activities — my enjoyment becomes shallow. I don't have the time to savour what happens. Leaving space in my day, rather than cramming it full, means I feel more able to stop and chat when I meet people. I feel more open to the small, immediate pleasures of the moment. I am more likely to be moved or changed by what happens to me.

Your Money or Your Life

The book that galvanized the modern voluntary simplicity movement is *Your Money or Your Life*.[1] In the following sections I will give a brief summary of some of the key concepts of the "Your Money Or Your Life" program. It is intended only as an introduction. Dominguez and Robin's book is excellent — comprehensive, well-organized, and thought-provoking. If you are serious about changing your relationship with money, do the full program set out in their book. If listening is a better way for you to learn, the program is also available as a workshop in audiotape format.[2] A website at **newroadmap.org** provides information on study guides, recommended reading, and study groups.

If I have to work to earn money, every time I buy something I am in essence trading some of my time and energy for something else. Voluntary simplicity is about becoming what the old Yankees would have called a "canny trader." I will only make trades when what I receive in the transaction offers me high fulfillment for the amount of my life energy that purchase represents. Whenever I am offered a trade where what I would receive isn't worth the amount of my life energy it costs, I will say "no."

Put that way, most people will say, "Yeah, of course. I already do that. At least, most of the time I do." I thought so too — until I completed the "Your Money or Your Life" program. In the next two years, my monthly expenditures dropped by more than half. Most people who complete the program see a drop in their expenditures afterwards — some more modest than mine, and some much larger.

I didn't have a budget to follow. I didn't deny myself things I wanted. There was no sense of deprivation. I didn't feel poor. I just stopped making bad trades.

Far from feeling constrained, I felt more freedom. I had more money available for the things that really mattered to me because I was no longer spending money on garbage purchases. I was able to save money so that my money began making money for me; every six months it sent me a cheque.

What's Your Time Really Worth?

The core of the "Your Money Or Your Life" program is a three-stage monthly review process. The first step is to personalize the "time is money" idea. Your official hourly rate of pay is not an accurate measure of what your time is worth because not all of your work-related time is paid, and not all of your gross pay makes it into your hands.

The easiest way for most people to do this step is to use a pay stub that covers a typical pay period. (If you are self-employed you will base your answers on a typical month's earnings and expenses.) To determine your real hourly wages you must first determine your real workweek. To your official work hours for that pay period add the following:

✦ Commuting time
✦ Unpaid overtime
✦ Time getting ready for work
✦ Time cleaning up after work
✦ Decompression time after work
✦ Any unpaid work done at home

The total is your actual work-related hours for the pay period. Next, to determine your actual net earnings, take the gross pay on your pay stub, add any tips or gratuities you received during the pay period, and subtract the following:

✧ All income and payroll taxes (from your pay stub)
✧ Union dues and professional fees (from your pay stub)
✧ The cost of commuting over that pay period
✧ The cost of work clothes prorated for that time (Estimate how much you spend on work clothes in a year, and divide that amount by the number of pay periods in a year.)
✧ Any other employment-related expenses

Now divide your actual net earnings by your actual work-related hours. The result is what an hour of your life energy is worth. This is what you really earn per hour.

When I figured out my real hourly wage, it was less than half of my official hourly wage. While finding out my true hourly wage was a humbling experience, it definitely reduced the temptation to try to buy time with money.

Tracking Monthly Income and Expenditures

The second step in getting a handle on money is to learn exactly where your money goes. To do that you'll need to keep track of every penny you earn and spend for the next three months, sorted by category. You can begin with a fairly standard array of categories — rent, telephone, medical/dental, groceries, bank charges, etc.

I found the easiest way to keep track of my expenditures was to keep receipts for everything I purchased. Unreceipted expenditures I would jot down on a scrap of paper. I stored all receipts in my wallet. Twice a week I input all this information into a home accounting program on my computer. Other people put all their receipts into category envelopes and total them later in a ledger.

Simply totalling and categorizing my expenses helped me understand better where my money was going. There were a number of surprises: how expensive it is to own a car, how quickly the cost of restaurant meals mounts up. I found the process of tracking my expenditures so useful I continue it to this day.

The Monthly Review

The third and final stage of establishing a financial feedback loop involves putting together the previous two steps. At the end of each month, subtotal each of your expense categories and convert the resulting dollar amount into hours of your life energy using the real hourly wage you determined above. Then ask yourself, Was what I received in this category worth the number of hours of my life energy it cost? (Sometimes it's necessary to review all the transactions in a particular category to remind yourself exactly what each category includes.)

Next to each category, mark a plus sign if you received high fulfillment relative to the money spent. Mark a minus sign where the fulfillment you received was not worth the hours of your life energy expended.

Sometimes it helps to break down larger categories into subcategories. For instance, when I looked at my "dining" category, it included full restaurant meals, but it also covered cups of tea with friends. These are very different experiences. Another person might want to break out "workday restaurant lunches" from restaurant eating because workday lunches are a significant expense on their own and have a different purpose from recreational dining.

Keeping receipts can be useful, at least for the first few months, so you get a detailed breakdown of some of your larger expenditures. If you wonder, "How could I possibly have spent $187 on groceries?" you can check back and see.

Most financial software creates transaction reports that list all of your specific purchases, sorted by category. I found that looking at transactions rather than categories gave me some hints about how to avoid purchases I would later regret. I found, for instance, that lingering over coffee with a friend cost little and typically had high value. Eating a full restaurant meal after work because I was too tired to cook was typically low in fulfillment.

I also began noticing behavioural clues that indicated what would turn out to be low-fulfillment expenditures for me. I was more likely to make poor trades of life energy when I was feeling tired or unhappy. A disproportionate number of my low-fulfillment expenditures had been paid for by credit card. As I came to recognize what kinds of buying circumstances were high risk for me, I became better able to avoid low-fulfillment purchases.

The point of rating your expenditures in terms of their fulfillment value is not to beat yourself up with the information (No shame/No blame is the prime directive), but to flag for yourself what kind of expenditures feel like poor trades in retrospect. Generally, after I had one or two experiences of thinking, "Oh, that wasn't worth it" when I made a particular type of expenditure, the next time that kind of purchase opportunity arose I immediately thought, "No, I don't *want* to buy that. It's not worth it." I did not feel deprived — I just had a sense of being able to choose more wisely.

As you go over your expenses one by one, you can often find ways to eliminate or reduce particular expenditures. Sometimes it may involve recognizing bad trades between time and money. If eating lunch at a restaurant on workdays costs 1.5 hours of life energy, while making a lunch takes 15 minutes of time directly and the cost equivalent of 15 minutes of life energy, that's an hour each day of life energy you have freed for something else.

Sometimes just paying attention is enough to spur action. When I saw that I was paying $10 every month for bank service charges, it spurred me to find an account where there were no service charges if I kept $1,000 in my account.

If, from time to time, you consciously choose to spend more in areas that are high-fulfillment, or if you use some of the money you've saved for a Big Adventure (see Chapter Eight), it will strengthen your experience that voluntary simplicity is not about self-denial but about getting good value for your money.

Buyer's High

As I reviewed my monthly expenditures, I came to understand what Dominguez and Robin call "buyer's high." I could create a wonderful euphoria for myself, imagining all the good times I was going to have with this purchase, imagining making other people happy with it, imagining other people's reactions to my purchase. My fantasies were sometimes completely ungrounded. The object of my fantasy would see more use in five minutes of runaway imagination than the real item got in five years of ownership. Afterwards, it was sometimes like coming down from a drinking binge. I'd feel regret, embarrassment, and wonder what I could have been thinking.

I saw that whenever I let the decision to trade two, twenty, or two hundred hours of my life energy be unduly influenced by a fifteen-minute "buyer's high," I was showing the priorities of an addict.

Once I recognized the problem of buyer's high, I was able to avoid it without having to restrict myself to planned purchases. The bubble of buyer's high was pretty fragile. If I suspected a high was forming, a two-minute time out in the store washroom would bring me down to earth.

Steps to Financial Independence

If you find you are able to feel happier living on less, the road rises to meet you in two important ways. Not only is it easier to save money towards financial independence, but the amount your investments need to generate each month to cover your expenses also drops. You run faster towards the goal line, and at the same time the goal line moves closer.

There are several steps you can take to achieve financial independence quickly.

Establish Where You Are Now

List all your financial assets and liabilities. The difference between them is your net worth. (Step One of the "Your Money or Your Life" program offers a template for doing this.) What part of that net worth could be converted into paying investments? Do you have a cottage that's empty much of the year? Could it be rented out? Perhaps you have a sailboat you use so seldom you'd be further ahead to sell the boat, put the money into an interest-bearing investment, and use part of the interest to rent a sailboat when you need one.

Graphing your monthly income, expenses, and investment income can help make your progress towards financial independence more visible to you.

Eliminate Low-Fulfillment Expenditures

Tracking and reviewing your monthly expenditures for a number of months will help you clear out low-fulfillment expenditures from your life. For most people, eliminating the expenditures that in retrospect were not worthwhile is enough to generate a savings stream.

Frugality can take bargain hunting to a whole new level. My frugal friends have the fourth Thursday of each month circled on their calendars. That's when all the thrift stores in Courtenay have their "dollar" days. Last week, two of my frugal friends, Peter and Sue, gave me a nearly new charcoal-grey suit — worth probably $500 brand-new — that they couldn't resist when it cost a dollar.

Eliminate Debt

The interest rate charged on most debts — whether it's credit card debt, car payments, or your home mortgage — is typically higher than the after-tax earnings of most investments. Each debt you eliminate removes the costs of servicing that debt from your monthly expenditures, which makes it easier to save in the future. (The main exception to this rule is tax-sheltered savings — 401Ks in the US, RRSPs in Canada — which sometimes confer a tax benefit large enough to make them worth doing before debts are paid off.)

Maximize Your Earnings

Pay attention to maximizing your hourly earnings, rather than maximizing your hours. Make sure all your capital assets are generating as much income as they can. If your kids have left home, or if you have no children, how would it feel to take in a boarder? Alternatively, would a smaller house be easier to maintain? Which of your current possessions are low-fulfillment? How much do you spend each year maintaining and housing your "stuff"? Selling off what you rarely use will generate a certain amount of investment capital. If impressing the neighbours no longer feels like a worthwhile use for your life energy, maybe it's time to sell that expensive SUV and use the proceeds to buy a used compact car.

If You're Planning to Relocate, Do It Soon

Do you live where you are now only because of your job? Is there somewhere you want to live when you are no longer tied to that job? What will it be like if you not only leave behind, overnight, the central organizing agent for your life — your job — but also move to a new community where you hardly know a soul? Could you be setting yourself up to feel lost and lonely?

What if, instead, at age fifty or fifty-five you move to that place you've always wanted to live and work part-time at a job that has you out in the community meeting people? Wouldn't that make for a gentler, easier transition? Isn't it more likely by age sixty-five you'll feel at home in that new community?

David Foot, demographer and author of *Boom, Bust and Echo*, points out that the baby boom bulge makes certain trends almost inevitable. According to Foot, millions of North Americans are hoping to move from big cities to a small town or a rural area when they retire, which will lead to two consequences ten to twenty years from now. The first is that a glut of boomers trying to sell their big-city homes will likely depress real estate prices in large metropolitan areas. The second is that that same flood of boomers will inflate real estate prices in small-town and rural areas.[3]

Let's say you figure another $100,000 in long-term bonds will provide the interest income you want for financial comfort in years to come. You save $10,000 per year for the next ten years. But by then your city home is worth $60,000 less, and your country dream home costs $60,000 more. You may be further ahead to move right now.

For those planning to settle in a new community, even if you're doing it at fifty rather than waiting till you're sixty-five, there's a looming danger of feeling isolated after such a change. Before you move to a new place, scout out the community for recreational and social opportunities. Find part-time work you can do. Think about how you plan to make yourself useful in that new place.

Eighteen months ago, at age fifty-eight, Jon Toogood sold his financial planning business in Winnipeg. Before he moved to the Comox Valley, he set up part-time work for himself. Jon's wife, Marguerite, became active with the Newcomer's Club within a week of arriving in the Valley. "In a new place, people won't come knocking on your door," she says. "You've got to go out and get involved." The transplanted couple quickly became connected with the Living Hope church, a brand-new and growing congregation. Jon came to the Comox Valley prepared to use his Winnipeg experience with Habitat for Humanity to establish a Habitat affiliate here. By consciously seeking ways to involve themselves, Jon and Marguerite avoided the trap of isolation and quickly knit themselves into their new community.

Customize Your Own Path To Financial Freedom

Many people using the "Your Money or Your Life" program have been able, within ten years, to reach the "crossover point," where their monthly income from savings exceeds their normal monthly expenditures. This means forty-year-old baby boomers could be free of the need to work by the time they turn fifty.

For some older boomers, the cost differential of downsizing their homes may be enough to give them a bridging fund to tide them over until they can begin collecting a pension. Just as often, older boomers who have been saving for a self-funded retirement based on their previous spending pattern will find their retirement investments are already generating more than their expenditures once they embrace voluntary simplicity. Others can use the reduced expenditures resulting from voluntary simplicity as an opportunity to cut back to part-time or part-year work.

Dominguez and Robin recommend that rather than investing in stocks, mutual funds, or real estate, you put your savings in the long-term bonds of your national government. They argue that domestic bonds have several advantages. When you own bonds, managing your investments costs little or nothing compared to mutual funds or stocks. Bonds generate a dependable income stream for a long time. The income bonds generate is typically much higher than GICs or savings bonds, and you are not tied in for years — you can sell them at any time.

Government bonds are a safe investment. Governments make the rules, so a nation's government bonds are going to be the last investment vehicle to fail. Bond incomes are stable, so you can estimate with a fair degree of accuracy how much you would need to save to be free of the need to work.

An increasing number of people are also deciding to put at least some of their savings into either ethical investment funds or "green" funds that invest in environmentally friendly businesses.

Dominguez and Robin argue against the urge to build in a big hedge against inflation. They contend that inflation is often an overrated fear in North America because the way in which inflation is calculated tends to overstate increases in the cost of living. My experience, in ten years of tracking expenditures, is that my monthly expenses dropped rapidly for the first two years and have continued to inch downwards since. So far, at least, my increasing skill at frugality has more than offset ten years of inflation.

The other thing to remember is that being free of the *need* to work for money doesn't mean you *can't* work for money. I think the idea that you should never work a day in your life after you retire is a silly restriction to put on yourself. I personally plan to always be doing small bits of paid work. Why? Because in a world where so much is structured around trading things of market value, there are times when paid work provides access to more and better resources, or means you are taken more seriously. Besides, I keep seeing small-business opportunities that I figure would be fun. By continuing to do little bits of paid work, I don't feel helpless to control my financial future if either my circumstances or my desires change.

For Those Who Have Them: Pension Considerations

The rules of pension plans across North America are complicated and incredibly diverse. If you have a workplace pension plan and are contemplating any change to your work situation, it's a good idea to contact your personnel department to find out exactly how a change in your work status would affect your eventual pension.

You must sometimes balance a desire for freedom with the constraints of your particular pension plan. Some pension plans require a certain number of years of service before pension earnings are "vested" — if you leave too early, you could lose your pension.

. Some plans base your pension on your last five years of earnings rather than your best five years, which makes it expensive to work less in your final years of work. With such plans it is sometimes better to quit entirely and find part-time work with another employer.

Many pension plans will allow participants to begin receiving a pension before the age of sixty-five if a person's age plus years of service exceeds some magic number (often one hundred, but sometimes as low as eighty-five). Sometimes part-time workers continue to accrue full years of service, in which case working less will modestly reduce the size of your pension, but will not change the date at which you can begin receiving it. If your pension plan prorates years of service for part-time workers, working less will have less impact on your eventual pension, but will push back the time when you can begin collecting it. A few pension plans will allow older workers dropping back to part-time to "top up" contributions to their pension plan so that working less will affect neither the size of their pension nor the date at which they become eligible to receive it.

Quitting your job will stop your years-of-service clock, which will push back towards sixty-five the time when you can begin collecting a pension from your workplace. Most plans will allow all participants to start collecting a pension at age sixty-five, regardless of years of service, once the minimum time requirement for vesting has been met.

Most human resource managers can give you a rough dollar estimate of how your pension would be affected by any change you are considering. If you're gritting your teeth waiting around to "max out" your pension, you should find out exactly what you're waiting for. That last five years may only add $200 a month to your pension. Capital gains from selling your home and moving to a smaller community might easily generate more than that in investment income right now.

Unhooking Self-Worth from Net Worth

So far we've been relating to voluntary simplicity only as a practical matter of getting value for your money. However, money in our culture also has emotional hooks that are worth our attention.

The constant message of advertising — that important people and "winners" have to own this or that status symbol — is part of the reason so many North Americans aspire to riches. Advertising constantly encourages us to feel good about ourselves by feeling superior to other people, by basing our self-worth on what we own rather than who we are. However, any self-worth that comes from being "better than," by definition separates me from other people. Self-worth based on being better than others is also inherently shaky in that no matter how much I have, or how often I win, there will always be someone a step higher than I am in the pecking order.

I've had a number of years of simple living to get used to the idea that my worth is the same whether I drive a Ferrari or a bicycle. Still, I'm not immune to our cultural programming. I noticed it most recently when I took the train and a city bus to a conference where I was giving a keynote address. There's something about getting up to speak in front of a large group of strangers that always shakes my self-confidence a little. On the bus I felt even shakier than usual. Then I clued in to what was happening. The normal shtick for keynote speakers is that the organizers fly you to the conference city, and a taxi or limo whisks you to the conference site itself. Without realizing that I was doing so, I had been using that VIP treatment as a crutch to fend off self-doubts at those moments.

If you've had a big income for a long time and been able to throw money around and impress others with your clothes, your car, the expensive restaurant meals you buy, or your $4,000 sound system, you may need to do some inner work to unhook your self-worth from your net worth. And you may need to find some different bricks to support your sense of worthiness.

Where does your sense of self-worth come from? Does it come from thinking of yourself as a winner? Is it hooked into some socially defined image of success? Or does it come from being a good person? I offer that as a choice because the energy and effort involved in trying to claw your way into the wealthiest 1 percent of America probably won't leave you much time for being an honest and caring human being.

North American culture has made it a virtue to aspire to great wealth. Wealthy wannabes are labelled as ambitious, as "go-getters." Even the human potential movement has given its blessing to the idea that seeking wealth is admirable and you should go for what you want.

There's plenty of sociological research that says aspiring to be like people who have more than you have will provide you with, at best, temporary highs. There's clear evidence that such ambition is a prescription for unhappiness and does not generate lasting satisfaction. Psychologist Tim Kasser has been conducting research on materialistic values for many years, and he summarizes the evidence: "Strong materialistic values are associated with a pervasive undermining of people's well-being, from low life-satisfaction and happiness, to depression and anxiety, to physical problems such as headaches, and personality disorders, narcissism and antisocial behavior."[4] To put it bluntly, trying to keep up with the Joneses is far more likely to make you sick than happy.

If you seek your sense of worth in loving relationships, in service, in personal integrity, you're far less likely to think you need to wear certain clothes or drive a certain car to be worthwhile. Sometimes, in this process, you may also find yourself shifting your friendship circle and gravitating towards people who value people more than things.

Finding Your Peers in the Global Village

Due to the effects of advertising and the fantasy world of television, it's easy to be rich in North America and feel poor. Sociologists report that most Americans believe the average American has considerably more wealth than the average American does.[5]

One method that I have found useful for developing a new relationship with wealth is to consciously change my reference group. Several books helped me through this process: Juliet Schor's *The Overspent American;* John de Graaf, David Wann, and Thomas Naylor's *Affluenza;* and Alan Durning's *How Much Is Enough?* (De Graaf also produced two wonderfully funny and insightful PBS videos: *Affluenza* and *Escape from Affluenza.)*[6]

Another useful therapy for North Americans is to read about life in the Third World. Fiction can be every bit as powerful as non-fiction in this regard. Try the novels of Rohinton Mistry or Arundhati Roy, for example. On a per person basis, the average yearly income of an American is sixty-five times that of half of the world's population.

For many people, travel to other countries helps them understand how much material wealth we have in North America. Travellers and overseas volunteers often come back from India or Indonesia appalled by the wastefulness and the excess of the North American lifestyle. When I was travelling in back-country Mexico — a rich country by Third World standards — I found myself asking how I could ever feel "deprived" about not owning something. It was also a reminder that these very poor people were clearly still capable of being happy.

Our good fortune in North America has become invisible to us.

We live in a place of peace, without raw sewage in the streets, where most people don't have to worry about going hungry — these are major blessings. Even the tragedies of September 11, 2001, were but a minor misfortune when we look at what has happened to the citizens of Cambodia, East Timor, Rwanda, or Somalia. "Get a grip" they would tell us. Obesity kills more North Americans every week than terrorism has in the past ten years.

Another way to change your reference group is to imagine how your ancestors would see your life. Even the poorest people in North America today have blessings that only kings and queens would have had two hundred years ago. To make this point at workshops, I like to lead a guided "Ancestors' Gathering" visualization (see Appendix A). People who have done this visualization report that it has sensitized them to the everyday blessings we take for granted.

Stepping Off the Treadmill

Once we understand the abundance in which we live — that we truly do have enough already — we can really begin to break free in the second half of life. We're free to spend our days doing something more interesting, more uplifting, and more fun than scrabbling after the almighty dollar. In his poem "My Symphony," William Henry Channing succinctly described this spiritual dimension of voluntary simplicity more than a hundred years ago:

> To live content with small means; to seek elegance rather than luxury, and refinement rather than fashion; to be worthy, not respectable; and wealthy, not rich; to study hard, think quietly, talk gently, act frankly; to listen to the stars and birds, to babes and sages; to bear all cheerfully, do all bravely, await occasions, hurry never. In a word, to let the spiritual, unbidden and unconscious, grow up through the common. This is my symphony.

CHAPTER SEVEN

Put Work In Its Place

The other major impediment to freedom most North Americans feel at mid-life is the time famine of the OverWorld. If at age forty or fifty or sixty you are feeling done in by work, it's time to say "Enough Already."

It may not be *immediately* possible to make the changes you want in your relationship to work. Still, you can at least begin moving towards what you want. Sometimes you don't need an immediate transformation to restore calm, but simply to put a liberation plan in place so that you can see yourself progressing towards your goal.

There's a built-in tension between wanting a balanced relationship with work and wanting to achieve the freedom of financial independence. After people have completed the "Your Money or Your Life" program, they often begin saving quickly. As debts disappear, they can save more rapidly, and once savings begin generating their own income, it becomes even easier to save, even on a less than full-time income.

In today's tight economy, sometimes your best option for quickly saving money involves staying full-time in your current job for a few more years. This is particularly true if your employer refuses your request to work less and you have few other options. The voluntary simplicity key will unlock the overwork box if you are patient and persistent. Once your debts are gone and you have some investment income, you'll have many more options.

Nonetheless, there are sometimes compelling reasons for putting work in its place before you are as ready as you would like to be financially:

- ✧ If you or your spouse are having major health issues, working less may be essential to your survival.
- ✧ Big Adventures (see Chapter Eight) are sometimes easier to imagine at age fifty than at sixty-five, and what we do at fifty expands the scope of what seems possible at sixty-five.
- ✧ If you want to live in a new place when you no longer need to work for money, it may serve you financially — and socially — to move now.
- ✧ In a time of unprecedented environmental crisis, you may feel called to do something different with your life. Maximizing your income may seem less important than doing what you can to protect the planet.
- ✧ Sometimes a job has grown so old and boring that it is time to move on, regardless of what it costs.

Another possibility, if you don't feel ready to make any permanent changes just yet, can be to test the waters with what Bob Buford calls the Half-Time Break.[1]

The Half-Time Break Option

If there's some big adventure you've always fantasized about, or a special one-time opportunity that comes your way, taking several months' leave from your current job to pursue that adventure can sow the seeds for bigger changes later.

When I talk with people who have taken a half-time break, they report several benefits:

✧ They got to do something they really wanted to do.
✧ Time away gave them a valuable new perspective on themselves and their world.
✧ One adventure often created both the appetite and the
   courage for more.
✧ Sometimes the adventure itself gave people information about
   where they wanted to go next in their lives.

Employers were often surprisingly accommodating in granting one-time leaves of absence to long-time employees, particularly when the time off was for something adventurous like sailing from Alaska to Mexico, or for something noble like doing AIDS education in Africa. To be more accurate, it's not so much that the organizations themselves were supportive as that middle managers often had the authority to authorize such leaves and did so when a vicarious sense of adventure captivated them.

   A half-time break can give you a valuable time out from your current life while allowing you to retain whatever financial and emotional security your job offers. It may also give you the clarity you need to make more lasting changes in your relationship to work.

Shrinking Your Current Job

When you reach the place of feeling financially and emotionally ready to reduce the amount of time you spend working, often the easiest and most elegant way to work less is to downsize your current job.

   If you've already made verbal requests to work less and been turned down, do not despair. There may still be ways to get what you want. Some years ago I was the executive director of Work Well, a small non-profit organization that, among other things, helped individuals negotiate reduced work-time options with their employers. We helped our clients design propositions that were win-win opportunities for themselves and their employer, and to produce organized, written proposals to argue their case. Our experience was that employees who took these steps were far more likely to get what they wanted than employees who made only verbal requests to work less. Written proposals also increased the success rate of those applying for a leave of absence to take a half-time break.

Eventually I wrote a how-to book for people that my agency could not serve directly because they lived too far away. *Put Work in Its Place: How to Redesign Your Job to Fit Your Life* is a unique and useful resource for negotiating a new work schedule for yourself.[2] In this section I'll give you the abridged version of *Put Work In Its Place*.

Is Shrinking Your Job the Best Alternative?

Before looking at how to shrink your job, there are a couple of important issues to consider first.

Do you like your job? If the only problem with your job is that it is too much of a good thing, working less will make a good job better. If your job feels ho-hum but bearable, shrinking it might still have value as an interim step to something new, especially if it gives you the time you need to train for a new career or to explore small business options. A half-time break could achieve the same end by helping you clarify where you want to go next. On the other hand, if you've come to *hate* your job, or there's something else you would really, really rather be doing, it's probably kinder to both yourself and your employer to leave your old job entirely.

When you no longer need to work for money, where do you want to live? If you always imagined yourself retiring to cottage country or the small town where you grew up or somewhere near the ocean, is it wise to wait until you leave the workforce entirely to do that? We saw in Chapter Six how there could be both a financial and a social advantage to moving sooner rather than later.

If, for either reason, it won't work for you to remain in a down-scaled version of your current job even temporarily, then skip ahead to the **Other Choices** section. Otherwise, carry on to learn how to put work in its place.

What Can You Afford?

If you've been tracking monthly expenses on the "Your Money or Your Life" program, you probably have a good idea of how much you need to earn from your job to keep the bills paid and achieve your saving goals. If not, spend time going over your bills for the past few months to determine the minimum amount of money you would need to earn each month from your job. When you have this figure, divide it by your current take-home pay and multiply the answer by the number of hours per week you currently work. That will give you a rough idea of the work-time reduction you can now afford.

If the reduction that results from this calculation is too small to satisfy you, you can try working on the problem from the opposite direction. Divide the number of hours per week you would prefer to work by the number of hours you currently work, and multiply the result by your current take-home pay. This will give you a rough approximation of the take-home pay you would receive for your preferred workweek. Fit this figure into your current monthly income and expense figures to see what short-fall results.

Now go back over your monthly expenditures to see where you might be able to reduce your expenses further. Brainstorm for ways to increase your income. Weigh what you'd have to give up against what you'd gain.

When you work less, there will be both savings and added costs. Savings typically include reduced taxes, lower commuting costs, and less money spent on restaurant meals. On the expense side, recreation costs may increase when you have more leisure time, and sometimes you'll be required to pay more for employee benefits. Savings are generally greater than the added costs, but if you don't have all the numbers, assume it's a break-even proposition.

If you end up deciding that you can't afford to work any less than you are now, don't despair. There may still be ways to lighten your load (see the **What Are Your Options?** section).

When you have a workable trade-off between what you want and what you can afford, it is useful to consider what form of time off suits you — one day a week, six months a year?

What Form of Free Time Do You Want?

What do you want to do when you have more free time? Is it most important to reduce the daily overload in your life? Would full days or full months off work be more appropriate for your needs?

Some activities (i.e., gardening, vigorous sports, courses that require intense concentration) are best suited to short periods of regular daily practice. A shorter workday leaves more room for these kinds of short, frequent activities. If your current workday leaves you too drained to do more than watch TV after work, a shorter workday can help insure that you still have energy left for your non-work life. The biggest disadvantage of shortening your workday is that it generally won't reduce the time you spend getting to and from work, which can be an important consideration for those who have a long commute.

Full days off work will reduce the time you spend commuting. They're also advantageous for activities that involve lengthy preparation or travel time. Making pottery or stained glass is not a project you can easily pick up or put down. For camping or sailing trips, it helps if you can extend the weekend by adding Friday or Monday. Recreational facilities are often less crowded on weekdays. A shorter workweek doesn't reduce workday stress, but it can enable you to fully recover and relax between workweeks. Some people use a day off during the week as their errand day, so when the weekend comes they're free to relax and play.

For other people, the things that relax and energize them require larger blocks of time. It can take weeks of camping before some people really relax. Longer periods of time off are required for travel, particularly travel overseas. The drawback of taking your time off in big chunks is that it doesn't reduce day-to-day stresses. The best outcome would be that you recharge your batteries periodically.

While it is occasionally possible to negotiate more than one form of time off, employers are usually less resistant if you ask for only one form of work-time reduction. It's useful, therefore, to figure out which form of time off best suits your needs before attempting to redesign your job.

What Are Your Options?

When you ask to reduce the size of your job, it is helpful to know how your organization will label your particular work-time request, because the rules by which your benefits and seniority are calculated may depend on how your work-time reduction is categorized. Before you start redesigning your job, make a quick visit to your human resources department to find out what scheduling options your employer currently offers and what the guidelines are for those options.

Permanent Part-time is the common name given for regular and substantial cuts to working time. Most organizations have policies about how many hours per week or year you need to work to retain full benefits and/or count as full-time for pension purposes. They also have a scale that shows how benefits change if you work less than that magic number.

Phased Retirement arrangements are offered by some employers to assist or encourage shorter work times in the years preceding full retirement. Sometimes this assistance takes the form of maintaining full benefits for older part-time workers. Some organizations continue making full-time pension contributions for senior workers who drop back to part-time. Phased retirement schemes are extremely common in Europe, but in North America only a few multinational firms and some public sector employers offer this option.

Job Sharing is an attractive option for people who want to cut their workweek in half. (You'll also occasionally see situations where three employees share two jobs.) It may meet with less employer resistance than permanent part-time because it handles the issues of relief staffing and has built-in mechanisms for maintaining continuity. Job-sharing partners can share the workday, the workweek, or the work year, so it provides time off in a variety of forms. (I have seen situations where job sharers who work half-weeks most of the year will switch to working alternating weeks during the summer so as to create more "vacation" weeks.) Job sharing can be a complicated option to put in place. Barney Olmsted and Suzanne Smith's *The Job Sharing Handbook* is a helpful guide.[3]

Leaves of absence, also called "personal leave" or "leave without pay," is the name most organizations use to describe taking weeks or months of time off. The longer leaves needed for a half-time break usually go under the name "extended leave."

Most organizations have rules about how much time you can take off — and how often — without having to pay extra for your employee benefits. Sometimes people who want only small reductions in work time — an extra day off a month or an extra few weeks off a year — will do better in terms of employee benefits by calling it "personal leave" rather than going to permanent part-time status.

V-time, or Voluntary Reduced Work Time, is a time/income trade-off scheme that may be ideal if you can only afford a small reduction in income. V-time programs typically allow work-time cuts as small as 2, 5, or 10 percent. V-Time is more flexible than most work options in that you can take your time off as a mixture of part-days, full-days, and full weeks. V-Time is still relatively rare but is so flexible that it's worth asking your human resources department if it's available in your workplace.

Banked Overtime — choosing to take your overtime as extra days off instead of being paid for it — can be a way to get extra days or weeks off work for a relatively small loss in income.

What if you can't afford to reduce your paycheque at all? You still have options. If you spend a lot of time commuting there are a number of ways to reduce your travel time.

Flexitime — sometimes called flextime — is widely available. You work the same number of hours, but by shifting them earlier or later in the day you can perhaps miss the rush hour or make better transit connections.

Compressed workweeks are another way of reducing commuting time. Compressing five days into four usually creates a workday that is too long. A common variant is called a nine-day fortnight or a modified workweek, in which an hour is added to your regular workday in return for an extra day off every second week. I have seen cases where working that extra hour pushes people far enough off the rush-hour peak that their daily commuting time drops by forty minutes, so the net increase in their workday is small in terms of the reward earned.

Telecommuting, or working from home, can also cut commuting time. If most of your work is done on the computer or the phone, working from home part of the week will free you of both the time and the expense of commuting. The general feedback I've received from telecommuters has been that two or three days of telecommuting per week is optimal; more than that and they start to miss the social contact of the workplace and feel out of touch.

Designing a New Work Schedule

Before you redesign your job, it is useful to spend a little time studying it.

✦ What are the sub-tasks that make up your job?
✦ How many clients and workmates are you regularly in contact with?

✧ How much of the information needed to do your job is in your head and how much is written down?

✧ How difficult would it be to replace you?

✧ How much of your job must be done at a particular time and how much can be done whenever you get around to it?

✧ How much of your job needs to be done at your workplace?

✧ If your job consists of "projects," how long do these projects typically last?

✧ Does your job involve plugging in one shift at a time? (Hospital nurses, store clerks, and assembly-line workers all have generic job structures in that anyone with the required skill set can plug in on any given shift.)

Before you can write up a proposal, you need to answer for yourself some basic questions:

✧ **Exactly what new schedule do you want?** When you develop a new schedule, remember that it should be simple enough for co-workers and your superiors to easily remember.

✧ **Who will be affected by the changes?** You should also consider how they will be affected and how you can minimize any disruptions for your co-workers and clients. Do you have co-workers who also want to work less? If so, perhaps you should be looking at submitting a collective proposal.

✧ **Who will do your work when you are not there?** How will you divide the work? It is easier for your supervisors to say "yes" if they don't have to find your replacement, and if the relief person you find is a known quantity. For job sharing in particular, a compatible partner is key to making it work.

✧ **How will you handle communication with your clients and co-workers?** Think about what office procedures need to be changed and how information will be transferred. How will others keep track of your schedule? Do staff meetings need to be held at a specific time so that everyone can attend, or is it enough to have someone responsible for taking notes for those not present?

✧ **How will the new schedule affect your seniority and employee benefits, particularly your pension?** You'll probably need to consult with your human resources department to determine the answer and to figure out what cost changes will result for you and for your employer.

✧ **What costs and savings will result?** Will extra office space be needed? Will benefit costs rise? Will your replacement be hired on a lower wage scale?

✧ **How could you make your new schedule advantageous to your employer?** Consider whether your new schedule will help with emergency or vacation coverage. Will it allow your organization to extend hours of service or provide better peak coverage? If your organization is going through layoffs, and particularly if several employees are wanting to work fewer hours, work-time reductions can be less painful and less expensive for your employer than layoffs.

Writing A Proposal

If you are the only person at your workplace wanting to work less, you'll probably need to write up an individual proposal. If it turns out that several of your co-workers also want to work less, you should consider either submitting a group proposal or, if you are unionized, having your union submit a proposal on your behalf.

When you write a proposal, think about how far up the chain of command it might have to go before it is approved. If you work for a big organization, it is probably a good idea to include enough detail about your particular job that people who don't know you or your job would have the information they need to make a decision. That being said, it's also wise to keep a proposal brief. Three to five typewritten pages is optimal. (There is a template for a work-option proposal in Appendix B.)

An organized, written proposal is your best tool for getting the work schedule you want. When you design the playing field, there's a better chance that the game will go your way. If you've done most of the research and planning, your supervisors can say "yes" without making more work for themselves. If your proposal anticipates and answers any concerns your supervisors might have, you will undercut their resistance. Written proposals are formal enough that they demand a response; you can't be put on hold indefinitely.

Sometimes your employer will make a counterproposal that gives you only a portion of what you want. You should be prepared for that possibility and have some idea what minimum conditions you would accept. It's also useful to have a Plan B to put in motion if you can't get what you want staying in your current job. The **Other Choices** section below should give you some ideas.

Other Choices

If your employer turns down your request for reduced work time in your current job, if it's inappropriate to stay where you are, or if your job has disappeared with a layoff notice, you still have a wide array of choices. If voluntary simplicity has put you close to financial independence, your range of choices is even larger. Though both unemployment and overwork are prevalent in North America, there are still millions of boomers who have been able to find or create working arrangements that give them a healthy balance between work and play. Here are a number of strategies to help you become one of them.

Shift Sideways

If your employer won't let you work less in your current position, is there a way you could shift sideways? Many firms are
now contracting out functions they used to perform in-house, as
well as hiring outside consultants for special project work and
employee training.

Many employers prefer covering maternity leave, sick leave,
and vacation time with experienced former staff, people they
know, rather than risking the lottery of hiring a temp worker.
Sometimes maternity coverage positions can segue into several
years as a member of a job-share pair.

For ten years, Don Clarke worked full-time as a health care aide
at Glacier View Lodge. The combination of full-time work and
working nights used to wear him down. "I used to crash and
burn regularly," he recalls. Last year, at age forty-seven, Don
shifted sideways to a "floater" shift: four hours at a time, four
days on, four days off. He also works occasional relief day and
evening shifts.

"We've had to cut back to live on less, but it's been well worth
it," Don reports. "It feels good just to have energy again, to not
feel tired all the time." He enjoys being able to spend more time
with his partner, Karen, and to put energy into his interest in
painting.

There's more than one way to shift sideways. A growing number of employers have discovered that offering work-time flexibility can be a powerful recruiting tool. Several of our Work
Well clients, when their employers proved inflexible on working
times, went to work for the competition.

A particularly satisfying way to shift sideways is what I call
"Turning your job on its head." Does your job push you to do
things you know are stupid, wrong, or inefficient? Why not use
what you know to create a job for yourself putting it right?

Many of our biggest, most entrenched systems — both public
and private — are environmental dinosaurs. If, for example, you

work in the building permit department of a typical North American city, the environmental impact of your job is probably worse than if you sold gas-guzzling vehicles for a living. To turn your job on its head, you could propose a part-time contract position for yourself researching environmentally friendly building materials and sewage treatment methods in order to update your city's building codes.

The problem is best summed up by that little placard found on the wall in many a workplace: "When you're up to your ass in alligators, it's hard to remember that your original intention was to drain the swamp." Organizations do not always respond warmly to swamp-draining proposals, but when they do, it can make for deeply satisfying work.

Set Firmer Boundaries

Another option, if you have reached the point where you are prepared to leave your job rather than put up with an oversized workweek, is to work only the hours you're paid for. Yes, it is likely that your work unit will fall behind on its work, but if you get laid off or fired for working the hours you are paid for, you are no worse off than if you quit. Perhaps you will come out ahead if a layoff makes you eligible to collect unemployment insurance while you look for a new job.

Among the most chronically overworked are the self-employed. It's hard to turn down work now when you're not sure you'll have enough — or any — work six months down the road. This seems a particular thorny problem for freelancers and contract workers.

One reasonably successful solution I have seen is to set up a rainy-day fund. Don't pay yourself for any work you do beyond what your preferred workload would be. Instead, collect income from any additional projects in a separate rainy-day account. The only time money leaves the rainy-day fund is when your actual workload falls below your preferred workload. The bigger your rainy-day fund gets, the safer you will feel turning down excess work.

I also know of freelancers, contract workers, and building contractors who have developed informal mutual-aid networks: I'll give you my overflow if you give me yours.

Small-business owners are often overworked. If you are in this group, you must learn to be dispensable. Sometimes the only way your second-in-command will learn to be as good as you are is if you let him or her learn the same way you did: through experience and by making mistakes.

The Single-Earner Option

If reduced workweeks are not a viable option, one of the ways a couple can reduce their collective stress load is to drop back to a single-earner lifestyle. The stay-at-home partner can take over shopping, cooking, cleaning, and house repairs so that the employed partner can relax when he or she comes home from work. Many North American workplaces have long-term leave options. If you both have such options available, you may be able to take turns being the one who stays at home, which will help avoid power imbalances between the earner and the non-earner. A single-earner model can be particularly helpful if you have aging parents who are needing more of your attention.

Doing What You Love

What do you love to do? Do you have a passion for model airplanes or spelunking or belly dancing? You can probably find a way to generate at least some money from doing what you love, whether by teaching, selling supplies, or offering some related service. If you're close enough to financial independence that you don't need a big income from your jobette, it can be a small or periodic business. (I have a friend who delivers bellygrams, for instance, as well as teaching belly-dance classes.) Not only will you be able to do something you love, but any supplies you buy or training you receive will be tax deductible.

I have a friend who loves to travel. Doug organizes canal tours in the south of France. He gets paid to show interesting people his favourite places. By limiting the travel work he does, it stays fun.

Marsha Sinetar's *Do What You Love, the Money Will Follow* can be a helpful guide for figuring out how to turn doing what you love into a source of income.[4] A surprising range of activities can create income, particularly if voluntary simplicity has reduced your needs to a modest level.

Follow-Your-Nose Work

My investment income is now a couple of hundred dollars a month less than my monthly expenditures, but I've discovered that I don't need a regular job to cover a shortfall that small. Little bits of work keep coming my way. Much of that work is either with friends or is associated with one or other of my interests. In either case, it hardly feels like work. I've been able to enjoy variety in the work I do, had the freedom to do a certain amount of travelling, and had the time I needed to complete this book.

One of the things that follow-your-nose work requires is the ability to revive old skills and learn new ones. In my experience, there have been huge differentials in income between my highest-paid and lowest-paid jobs, but I don't care, because I am working primarily for fun and interest.

Another alternative for people who don't need a full year's income is to make yourself available year after year as back-up staff during a business's rush season — sometimes putting in lots of hours over a short period — so you can be free for the remainder of the year.

Setting Up to Work Where You Want To Live

Moving to a smaller community can have both social and capital-cost advantages, but if your investment income doesn't cover all your expenses, you'll still have to find ways to earn a living. The good news is that part-time and part-year positions are often more common in smaller communities.

Between the opportunities offered by the Internet and the flexibility of telecommuting, you can occasionally find ways to live where you want and earn your money somewhere else. While this may hamper your ability to connect to a new community, it may still be a better option than not moving at all.

Micro-Businesses

One thing you will notice when you have more time is that the world is full of micro-business opportunities — market niches that are too small to attract the attention of big business. If you want a business that is small and will stay small, a micro-business can be ideal.

If you have nearly achieved financial independence, you may have the freedom to learn the skills needed for the micro-business of your choice or to build up a clientele gradually.

A volunteer interest can grow into a micro-business as well. I started teaching an eight-week course on heart health as a way to reinforce diet and exercise changes I had made for myself. Since then, teaching the course has become an enjoyable and rewarding way to get periodic infusions of cash while still leaving large chunks of my year free.

It can take a long time to develop expertise in the modern world. The exception to that rule is at the cutting edge of change. When something is new enough to be seen as experimental or alternative, it usually takes less time to learn as much as "the experts" do. If you are willing to take the time to educate yourself, you may be able to find and create work in the most innovative and exciting occupational niches more easily than in mainstream occupations.

However, when you are choosing a micro-business, remember that meeting everyday needs often works better than trying to get into the latest business hot spot. I have a friend who keeps bees. Murray's Apiary generates a modest income while getting Murray out in nature from time to time. "It's a throwback to my back-to-nature hippie days," he says.

'Somebody' Work

Is there a social or environmental need that grabs you by the collar? Maybe "somebody" should protect that special valley as a park. Maybe "somebody" should form a local credit union so we can make sure our savings stay here. Maybe "somebody" should establish a proportional representation voting system so that Canada and the United States might actually function as democracies. If you get tired of saying "somebody" should do something about your pet issue, perhaps it's time for you to become a "somebody."

It's unlikely that "somebody" work will make you rich. However, by relying on donations, foundation grants, and sales of cause-related publications and products, a great many people have been able to generate modest incomes working to do good in the world.

"Somebody" roles can emerge from the linkages we make. In his fifties, Vancouver Island resident David Stott was able to set up part-time, part-year work for himself by combining his experience as an organic farmer with his interest in anti-poverty activism. Seeing that long-term welfare recipients were frequently too isolated, too discouraged, and too fearful to be able to look for work or go back to school, David proposed a project that would act as an intermediate step. David's Garden Project taught long-term welfare recipients the basic skills of organic gardening.

Land and materials for the project were mostly donated. Governments provided wages for the staff and a transport stipend for the participants. At a minimum, all the people who participated in David's project improved their ability to feed themselves. Most participants were able to use the program as a stepping stone to either employment or further schooling. The program's success at helping people out of the welfare trap was such that David received government financial support to organize Garden Projects in two other communities. Reflecting on the circle of volunteers, donors, and supporters each Garden Project attracted, David says proudly, "Garden Projects didn't just nurture individuals; they also nurtured communities."

Adventures that Pay the Bills

Did you always wish that you'd gone off and worked for the Peace Corps or CUSO when you were younger? Do you still occasionally wish that you could go somewhere exotic to do something for others?

Perhaps you've reached the place where you can see that, once Social Security or CPP and/or a pension kicks in, you'll have enough income, and all you need to do in the interim is keep the bills paid.

In such situations, overseas volunteer work that provides room and board can function as a job. By renting out your home in North America and allowing your investment income to roll over, you can sometimes even save for retirement while volunteering — or at least build up a cushion of savings to make re-entry easier when you return.

All over the world, people want to learn to speak English. It only takes a few months to earn the necessary credentials to teach English anywhere in the world, and you don't have to know how to speak the language spoken by your students. Living in another country can be an excellent way for you to learn another language and earn an income while you're doing so.

There are also semi-volunteer options available. For example,

Experience Corps is a program in which mature individuals (over age fifty-five) work as teachers' aides in US elementary schools and receive a modest stipend (for more information see **www.experiencecorps.org**).

Back to School

Sometimes, to do what you want to do, you just have to go back to school. One thing to consider when choosing a second career is whether part-time or part-year options are going to be easily available when you finish your training. Some fields — like counselling, for instance — work well as part-time home businesses. Retired accountants usually have no trouble picking up extra bits of work in tax season.

Sometimes you can earn money as a student by, for example, working as a dorm chaperone or taking an apprenticeship. Many professors prefer to hire mature students as teaching assistants or to mark papers and exams.

The Other Half of Restoring Balance

Taming an oversized workweek can be a job in itself, requiring patience, persistence, imagination, and courage. But when you've succeeded in cutting your workweek down to size, the job of putting work in its place is only half done. You still have to correct whatever imbalances overwork has inflicted upon you. Fortunately, while shrinking your workweek may be a trying task, recovering your balance is a joy and pleasure, as you'll see in Chapter Eight.

CHAPTER EIGHT

Get a Life, Eh!

"Get a life!" is often the sarcastic rejoinder when a person exhibits the shrunken horizons of a life ruled by work. Once you've put work in its place, getting a life is both an art and a pleasure. It takes time and requires a delicate balance between letting it happen and steering the process a little.

You may already have a clear idea of what you want to do with your time once you cut your job down to size. Don't be in too much of a hurry. If you've spent years without enough free time, there may be quite a few horses inside you, all wanting to push out the gate at once.

Sleeping in, reading the books you never had time for, sharing play time with your partner, catching up on various unravelled corners of your life, seeing old friends . . . that may be as far as you get for the first several months, and it will feel delicious just the same.

In this chapter I'd like to focus on a first-aid level of recovering your balance. After you've got your feet properly underneath you, you'll probably want to pay some attention to lifestyle health issues (Chapter Nine). Eventually you'll need to pay more attention to the second half's Big Three: purpose, connection, and challenge (Chapters Three, Four, and Five). But first allow yourself the pleasure of feeling centred, balanced, and time-rich.

The possibilities that follow are just that: possibilities. Some will resonate with you. Some will have no appeal, at least not at the moment. Go to what draws you. The smorgasbord of choices is delightful, but part of the art of dining is knowing when to stop eating.

Reawakening the Body

Bioenergeticist Alexander Lowen has observed that it is a mistake to describe North Americans as "materialists." Materialists would enjoy the simple, immediate pleasures of life — the taste of good food, the feel of a silk shirt, the warmth of a wood fire — far more than most North Americans do. Rather than being materialists, he says, we are abstractionists, living in symbols and taking our pleasures from symbols and images.

Lowen even gives a name to our condition: anhedonia, or the inability to feel pleasure. People who live in their heads are cut off from the pleasure of the body and from its wisdom.

If years of stress have you living in your head, if it has turned food into fuel, if your body has forgotten how to really enjoy itself, it can be good therapy to invest some time in the simple pleasures of life. Walking, stretching, yoga, massage, dancing, making love, lying in the sun, savouring good food — anything that gets you back in your body will help reopen you to its wisdom.

I experience the food that I grow or gather differently from food that I buy. It feels more real as food, and I am somehow more intimately connected to it. When I make meals from scratch, or brew my own beer and wine, I recover some control over what goes into my body. I can save money while eating in ways that are healthier and tastier.

The experience of preparing food, and particularly the experience of preparing food for others, can be a concrete expression of creativity, love, and caring. Food is meant to be savoured and shared. The French have a much more satisfying attitude about food. Meals are an excuse to get together for hours of conversation and laughter.

Self Time

If work has taken up too much of your time for a long time, it can be a while before you start to get clear internal signals about what you really want for yourself. (If you're too busy for anything but work anyway, I suppose it's a blessing of sorts to lose touch with your heart's desires.)

Various disciplines of inward focus — for example, journalling, keeping a diary, meditation of any kind — can help you learn to listen for those signals. Meditative physical activities like yoga and Tai Chi can open us gently to ourselves. Sometimes making art or music takes us deeper into our self.

Spiritual practices in most religious traditions tend to help people develop an inward focus. Quiet time and time alone can provide space for long-suppressed wishes and feelings to re-emerge. We may need to experiment with things that gave us joy in the past in order to find out if they still have juice. Sometimes it is only by following our inner promptings that we can come to understand their wisdom.

Nature has a healing power for most of us. It operates on a different time scale, without hurry, and it reminds us of the sacred cycles of life. Little moments of wonder — a tiny bird, a sunset, the exuberant fecundity of an apple tree in autumn — remind us we are creatures ourselves, part of the wonder of nature, and that we have our own rhythms and our own song.

A Warning to Workaholics

One of our assumptions in North America is that the busier we are, the more useful and important we must be. But being busy can also become a way of hiding. If old traumas from childhood start to re-emerge, I can bury them with busyness. If a spouse leaves or a child dies, I can shut out the pain. If I feel fearful or despairing about the future of the planet, frenetic activity will numb those feelings.

If, in the past, you have used work to escape from distressing feelings or unfinished emotional business, be aware that you may have some homework to catch up on before you are really able to enjoy having space and time in your life. Also be aware that if you don't deal with the issues that drove you to work obsessively, you will probably find non-work ways to become obsessively busy all over again.

Many people alternate between using work and using alcohol or some other addiction to escape from distressing feelings. Reduce one escape route and the need for the other will grow. If you've been a workaholic and find yourself having more trouble with alcohol after putting work in its place, don't minimize the problem. Get counselling support for yourself.

Coping With the World's Craziness

There's one indirect advantage to the time famine of modern life: it makes it easier to ignore the craziness of the world. When you have more time, the misplaced priorities of the North American lifestyle will become clearer to you. You'll also have time to gather information about the consequences of those misplaced priorities. The Internet is full of websites on social and environmental issues like **www.alternet.org** and **informationclearinghouse.info**. There are some scary and depressing things happening in the world right now that don't make it to the TV evening news.

Having more time, and more information, can make it easier to sink into gloom about the future of the planet, but this makes you as much a part of the problem as those who are too busy to notice. I have struggled with this issue and have come up with some strategies to keep my balance.

First, I limit how much time I spend gathering information. The world is now so information-rich that gathering bad news can become a full-time job. I gather enough information to keep current, but not so much that I drown in it. When I can I spread information about important issues by writing to selected friends, via letters to the editor, and through queries to the mainstream media.

Second, I ask, What can I do personally in my own lifestyle decisions to be part of the solution rather than part of the problem?

Third, I look around for some proactive step I can take to be a force for change in the world. At the moment I can see no better intervention than to encourage my peers to unplug from the OverWorld — hence the book you are holding.

Finally, I deliberately pay attention to all the small beauties and pleasures of life and make sure I am kind and compassionate in my daily interactions. This immediate circle of sanity acts as a bulwark against the larger craziness.

Play Time

Play is one of the things that gets squeezed out of our too-busy lives. What activities did you enjoy when you were twenty or twenty-five? Were you once involved in little theatre? Have you always wanted to learn to jive? Maybe you've felt envious watching ballroom dancers or a cappella singers. Music, song, theatre, and dance are creative forms of play that connect us to other people. Birdwatching or wild-food gathering can add zest to a walk in the woods. Card games and board games are a great excuse to get together and laugh.

Sport that is playful connects us to other people while making exercise a pleasure. A little bit of play lightens and leavens life. It reminds us not to take the world too seriously.

Big Adventures

A Big Adventure can be a productive time out from whatever life you have had till now. Big Adventures also seem to loosen up the ground for other changes. Take a minute to close your eyes and think back over your life. Are there things you've always regretted not doing when you were young? Backpacking around Europe, say, or becoming a missionary in Africa, taking a degree in architecture, or forming a rock band?

In the first years of the second half of life you have a second chance to do whatever you didn't get around to earlier. If the longings you had then no longer move you, that's fine. Let them go, but don't lie to yourself. You're not too old.

What "someday" promises have you made to yourself? Someday I want to climb Mount Kilimanjaro. Someday I want to sail around Vancouver Island. Someday I'll learn to speak French and bicycle across the French countryside with my spouse. Someday I'll go camping with my grandson, to the lake where my grandparents took me as a child. Is there a novel you've had rattling around in the back of your head for years? What promises have you and your partner made to each other about what you'll do when you no longer have to work? Which of those "someday" promises has the most juice? What prevents you from doing it now?

If you have reached the stage where you can get by on follow-your-nose work rather than a regular job, be aware that Big Adventure opportunities will come knocking on your door — so be ready. More accurately, ideas that in the past you would have dismissed as pie-in-the-sky fantasies, suddenly have to be taken seriously.

As an example, I'll tell you what I've been doing in the past year. Last summer my friends Sue and Art started building a cob house, which was exciting because alternative building methods have long been a fascination of mine. (Cob is the temperate-climate equivalent of adobe, and as a building material it uses about 3 percent of the energy of most modern construction materials.) I volunteered to help, but Sue and Art took me aside and said they wanted more of my help than they felt comfortable asking me to volunteer. They wanted to pay me. (It was probably a good thing, in retrospect, because that income allowed me to take several months for writing.) The work was physically demanding, but it was a pleasure to work with good friends. Now that their home is up and occupied, I take pleasure in it each time I visit.

Last fall I spent a month in the Queen Charlotte Islands. My partner Adriana's daughter had bought a house there and was renovating it to be a bed and breakfast. The main floor needed tiling, a skill Adriana and I both happen to have. Adriana's daughter paid our travel costs, and we went and tiled her floors. It felt good to be able to help her and to leave our mark on her new home. Afterwards she dropped us off with a double kayak at Hotspring Island in the middle of Gwaii Haanas park. We had several days to explore that incredibly wild and beautiful country, with the hot springs to soothe sore muscles after a long day's paddling.

I'm currently racing to finish up the final editing of this book — an adventure in itself — because Adriana's cousin has offered us the use of an empty apartment in Spain for as long as we want it. In past years, three months in Spain would have been a pipe dream. Now it's an offer we can't refuse!

The specifics of what I did are not important; you might choose very different adventures. What's important is that with freedom comes a steady stream of opportunities to do what is exciting to you. In fact, I have to agree with what several people have told me: There can be so many opportunities that you need to learn to be selective so you don't end up feeling scattered.

Big Adventures can be scary, not least because your favourite fantasy could get mugged by reality. However, putting them off only makes them scarier and makes it easier to decide you're "too old" for that sort of thing. If your kids have left home and your health is good, there may be no better time than now.

Yes, you could teach English in Manila at age sixty-five or bicycle across the south of France or climb mountains. But if all you've done for the past twenty years is work obsessively and watch television, how likely is it to happen?

I don't think it is ageism to say that you are more likely to climb mountains at age sixty-three if you climbed the occasional peak when you were forty-eight. And you're more likely to bicycle across the south of France as a septuagenarian if you've had a history of such adventures than if you've never done it before.

A balanced life is not a static thing. Sometimes a big project will suck up large amounts of your time and energy, and whole sections of your world will feel a trifle neglected. Or a Big Adventure may take you away from your home community for months at a time. As the Greeks used to say, Moderation in all things, including moderation.

Travel

Many of the Big Adventures people promise themselves for retirement involve travel. It's why people may think they'll need a lot of money to be comfortable in retirement.

Travel can be addictive consumption par excellence. "That was the year we did Greece and Turkey," you'll hear travel addicts say. If you see twelve cities in fourteen days, it's just doing North American affluenza someplace else. Consuming the world as a lifestyle also leaves compulsive travellers disconnected from their home communities. On the other hand, a few months of leisurely travel can be the perfect time out for a recovering workaholic.

Strangely enough, the less money you spend while travelling, the more likely you are to be changed and enriched by the experience. To really understand another culture, you need to stick around, get to know people, learn the language, eat what they eat. When you stay somewhere, you can start to make friends, not with other tourists, but with the locals. If you take the time to learn about a place before you go, perhaps even learn the language, you're in a much better position to make a connection. And doing so means the adventure begins even before you leave home.

The longer you stay away, the more you'll learn how to live frugally in that new place. A full month's lodgings might cost the same as seven single-night rentals. You can earn more renting out your Canadian or American home than it will cost you to live like a local in many parts of the world. If you make your travel adventures a third as often but stay three times as long — and use surface transport where you can — frugal travel is also much less costly for the environment. If you look around, you will see many ways to travel inexpensively:

✧ There are several house-swap services on the Internet. Sometimes travellers will even swap cars and take care of each other's pets.

✧ Another option is to join SERVAS (**www.servas.org**), an international organization of volunteer hosts. The purpose of SERVAS is not cheap travel but rather the creation of international understanding by building friendships between people of different cultures. As a SERVAS host you don't necessarily have to leave home to enjoy another culture. People from distant and exotic lands will come to visit you as often as you go visiting abroad.

✧ Most of the world's "youth" hostels are now open to people of all ages.

✧ WWOOFing (**www.wwoof.org**) is a way to have a working holiday. The initials stand for Willing Workers On Organic Farms. WWOOFers do four hours of farm work a day in return for room and board. They will often arrange to hopscotch across the country of their choice with a series of placements they booked before leaving home.

✧ Travel and service are not mutually exclusive. Aid organizations in Third World countries need a surprising range of skills. If you don't happen to have a skill they require, but do have the time as a volunteer to take training, you can find ways to make yourself useful in a place you want to visit.

✧ Some service clubs have international links. The Rotary International offshoot of Rotary Clubs has development-assistance projects in several of the world's poorest countries, working in partnership with local Rotarians in those countries.

<u>Couple Time</u>

Many years ago I went to a delightful workshop by Mario and Lila Bartoletti called "An Affair Within a Marriage." Mario began the workshop by recounting how he had come close to starting an affair with a co-worker. At the last minute he backed out, but not before noticing how differently he treated his prospective lover than his wife. He and his wife had become "Mom" and "Dad" in their relationship. With his would-be lover he went to beautiful places. He dressed up. They ate sensual foods together in an intimate setting. When he was with her he cleared all the busyness of do-do-do life out of his head and focused solely on her. He treated her as if she was special and his time with her was special.

He realized that he enjoyed the different attitudes and behaviours that were associated with his nascent affair. He also became aware that those attitudes and behaviours were conducive to intimacy. And he saw that there was nothing except habit and familiarity preventing him from behaving that way with his wife.

Mario and Lila began a conscious exercise with each other. They asked themselves, If this person and I were not long-term spouses but brand-new lovers, how would we treat each other? They began doing more of the things that people do when they are courting, and they felt more like lovers again as a result. Even their children noticed the difference. Mario described how his son came in one day as he was dressing up to go out and said, "Hot date tonight, eh, Dad!"

If there's a significant other in your life, you may want to ear-mark some of your new-found time for that relationship. Between the demands of parenting and the stresses of the OverWorld, many couples feel somewhat estranged at mid-life. Be aware too that if multiple major issues have been kept on hold for a long time in a too-busy life, those issues can emerge all at once when time pressure is released. Making more time for each other, par-ticularly with the added privacy that is available after the kids leave home, can help a couple deal with whatever baggage they carry and restore intimacy to their connection.

Sexuality and Sensuality

I have to confess that when I was in my forties, sex got a little dull. It was less frequent, less exciting. Being a natural story-teller, I made up stories to explain what was happening — changing hormones, not a young man any more, that sort of stuff. So I was really surprised in my fifties to find myself enjoy-ing sex more — and more often — than ever before.

If I had been further into my research about the second half of life, I probably wouldn't have been caught off guard. Many authors report that sex, like wine, gets better with age.

Theresa Crenshaw's book *The Alchemy of Love and Lust* offers one of the best overviews of sexuality throughout the life cycle. Cren-shaw says that when men and women are in their twenties, their biologies don't mesh well. They are "about as emotionally ill-suit-ed for one another as they will ever be but, as we all know, that does not discourage them from relentless pursuit of one another."[1] Twenty-somethings may think about sex a lot and want sex a lot, but they are often less successful at actually enjoying sex.

In our thirties, the biological and emotional match is better. For some couples, sex will be markedly better in that decade. Unfortunately, as the workweek has gotten longer and more intense, and as more families have adopted a dual-earner model, the twin pressures of parenting and overwork regularly stifle any opportunity for eroticism. In the counselling field, we refer to it as the TINS syndrome: Two Incomes, No Sex. TINS often continues into the forties.

For those of you still mired in TINS, don't lose hope. Here's what Crenshaw has to say about our fifties:

> For the first time in their lives men and women are perfectly matched sexually and emotionally — assuming they stay healthy and hold on to each other. A fifty-something couple can have all the romance and sex they've ever imagined and more. They usually have more time, less pressure and fewer worries — pregnancy is irrelevant, the children are gone and the work world is being managed better. Even more significantly, biology and maturity collude to bring men and women this age even closer.[2]

A sexual renaissance in the second half of life can continue for a long time. According to Theresa Crenshaw, "The bottom line on aging is this: Barring debilitating disease, there is no reason a man and woman can't enjoy love, romance, intimacy, and sex as long as they live."[3] In *The Virtues of Aging,* former president Jimmy Carter reports that his sex life with Rosalynn is better at seventy-something than it had ever been.[4] Eventually we may reach the point where our sex life is reduced to cuddling — but for those who maintain good physical health, this may not happen for a long time.

Yes, you say, a sexual renaissance sounds delightful. Where do I sign up? Only modest steps are required:

✧ **Make time and space for romance.** Stress is the enemy of eroticism. Be open to being pleasantly surprised.
✧ **Eat well.** The same diet that protects a man against heart disease (see Chapter Nine) will also reduce his risk of impotence.

✧ **Exercise.** Moderate exercise increases circulation to all parts of the body, including the sensitive parts. Losing weight can make you look and feel sexier.

✧ **Use it or lose it.** There's some evidence that if you are celibate for an extended period of time, your body's sexual responsiveness will atrophy. Theresa Crenshaw goes so far as to recommend that people who are single, widowed, or otherwise without a sexual partner should consider masturbating from time to time to keep their sexual functioning intact for a later date. Masturbation may also protect a man from prostate cancer.

✧ **Clear out whatever is in the way.** Resentments and unfinished business build up between a couple when they are too busy for too long. Romance can return when we deal with whatever issues have gotten in the way.

Self-Efficacy Skills

Self-efficacy is what psychologists call a generalized feeling of competence. We live in a society where it is tempting to become good at one thing and then use that one thing to buy everything else. But that one-pointed competence has a certain shakiness to it. Lose your job, lose your money, and suddenly you feel vulnerable.

Having some basic competence at a wide range of concrete, everyday skills gives a person a sense of solidness and security. There is a certain "I can handle it" self-confidence that comes from knowing a variety of basic skills: how to prune a fruit tree, how to tune a car engine, how to build a shed roof, how to give a child a passable haircut, how to navigate a boat in the fog.

Your grandchildren probably won't be terribly impressed by the fact that you were a leveraged buyout specialist. They're more likely to be swayed if you can play funny songs on the guitar, build a birdhouse, sew a Halloween costume, or make a lemon meringue pie.

If I am broadly skilled, it means I can probably make myself somewhat useful anywhere I go. I also know that whatever disaster happens in the world, I'll probably find ways to cope and help others. I can have small but regular feelings of making the world move in my direction without needing money as an intermediary.

In the world of full-time work it's easy to lose your self-efficacy skills, to buy what you need rather than making and doing things for yourself. Reclaiming the ability to meet your own needs directly will help you feel grounded, capable, and able to handle whatever life throws at you.

Chaos Control

Something that happens to most people who are too busy is their lives are often on the verge of unravelling. There are photographs spilling out of boxes next to empty photograph albums. Half-finished construction projects nag away in the background. The jungle in the backyard is barely under control. You wait too long to file for reimbursement of extended medical expenses and can no longer claim them. Storage closets are so randomly stuffed you end up buying things you already have because you can't find them. Tools or toys become useless because you forget routine maintenance or leave them too long in the rain. Keeping entropy at bay is a rearguard action. You are caught in a Catch-22: disorder causes stress, but re-establishing order in a time-starved life would be even more stressful.

I'm not a big fan of the perfectly ordered life. My experience is that people whose homes and workshops are models of perfect and complete order have small lives. Still, it is a form of self-care to have a certain minimum level of order in your physical world. It reduces stress. It reduces waste. It saves you the time and frustration of looking for things you can't find. Inner peace is difficult if your environment is in chaos. One of my favourite resources on chaos control is Julie Morgenstern's *Organizing from the Inside Out*. Morgenstern has a wonderfully practical step-by-step approach to making the unmanageable manageable.[5]

When you're living a hyper-fast lifestyle, it's easy to skip over what we're doing to the environment, to make it someone else's problem. It's easy to find yourself too busy to recycle, and the speed of life carries you into all sorts of habits that create waste and waste energy (buying take-out food in environmentally unfriendly Styrofoam containers, for instance).

When we truly realize what kind of world we are leaving to our grandchildren, it gets harder and harder to ignore the destructiveness of the North American lifestyle. Consciously living in ways that reduce waste and energy use — and maybe even finding ways to encourage others to do the same — becomes necessary to maintain peace of mind.

The Gifts of Time

In this chapter we have focused on first-order recovery from the imbalances created by the time famine. Giving yourself the gift of time can restore you to balance and centredness and can put play, pleasure, and adventure back into your life.

Most of us carry an additional legacy from the time famine: one or more unhealthy lifestyle habits. Left in place, this baggage of bad habits can sap both health and vitality. Another of the gifts of time is that it means we are in a better position to take good care of ourselves, as we shall see in the next chapter.

CHAPTER NINE

Invest in Vitality

Living in the OverWorld means that many North Americans reach mid-life with serious health risks, and sometimes with serious health problems. Once you've put work in its place and had a chance to recover a sense of balance in your life, it's probably a good idea to clean up any lifestyle health issues that might otherwise get in the way of a long and happy freedom.

I'm not suggesting that you become a lifelong neurotic about health issues — I hope you have better things to do with your time. But it could be worthwhile making health a major focus of your life for several months, and doing so sooner rather than later.

Lifestyle changes can have a surprisingly large influence on health and longevity. Looking at the issue of heart disease, for example, John Rowe and Robert Kahn comment, "In the famous Framingham Heart Study, if older individuals had been able to reduce their risk factors for heart disease, the men would have survived to 100 years of age and the women to ninety-seven years of age. And remember this: they would potentially have lived both longer *and* healthier lives" (italics in original).[1]

It does require a considerable amount of energy, attention, and time to put in place the foundation of a healthy lifestyle. Once that foundation is in place, however, it takes only small amounts of energy to maintain it — far less energy than it will take to deal with poor or declining health in years to come.

Why Sooner Is Better Than Later

Do you have "retirement resolutions"? Are you planning to lose weight, stop smoking, eat more carefully, or exercise more once you completely leave the workforce? While later is better than never for such changes, sooner is ever so much better.

Why is that so? It has to do with something called "reserve capacity." At age twenty your heart can pump twice as much blood as your body needs. Your arteries can carry double the blood your body requires. Your liver can remove twice as many toxins as your body produces. Most of your body systems have a reserve capacity of 100 percent or more. Reserve capacity represents how much room you have between that body system working well and systemic distress or breakdown. With each passing year, some of your reserve capacity disappears. If your lifestyle habits are good, you may lose 1 percent or less of your reserve capacity each year. If you've got bad habits, you could lose as much as 3 percent of your reserve capacity each year.

What does that mean? Well if you've had average lifestyle habits, your reserve capacity may have been dropping by 2 percent a year since you were twenty years old. By age fifty, your reserve capacity has dropped 2 percent a year for thirty years. With 60 percent gone, you've got 40 percent left. Switch to good but not saintly lifestyle habits at fifty, and the rate at which your reserve capacity disappears should fall to 1 percent per year or less. The 40 percent that remains is still enough to see you through from fifty to beyond ninety years of age before any red lights start appearing on your body's dash panel.

On the other hand, if you keep your bad habits for another ten years, your reserve capacity will shrink from 40 to 20 percent by age sixty. Switch to good behaviour then, and you won't be far past eighty years of age when the red lights start to flash. Wait till age seventy to make the changes and — whoops! — your reserve capacity is gone. You can live like a saint and it won't matter. Within a few years your body will be in a bad way.

Young people can get away with bad behaviour. You can thrash your reserve capacity down from 100 percent to 50 percent and you'll hardly know the difference. However, in your middle years, if you shrink your reserve capacity from 50 percent to zero, the matter will be brought forcibly to your attention. Don't wait to act on your retirement resolutions. Do it now.

That Little Talk from the Doctor

About five years ago, my then partner got the "your cholesterol and your blood sugar are both too high" warning talk from her family doctor. I knew from my last visit to the doctor that my numbers were better — but not terrific.

Her doctor recommended she read *Dr. Dean Ornish's Program for Reversing Heart Disease*. We read Dr. Ornish's book, and several others, and over the next year made major changes to our diet and exercise regimen. Working part-time gave us the time and energy we needed for making these changes. Within a year we had each lost 30+ pounds. Cholesterol and blood sugar readings dropped by a third for both of us, pulling them out of high-risk territory.

I also felt better: stronger, more energetic, more attractive. My body was better able to fight off colds and infections. Five years later those benefits are still with me.

Making major lifestyle changes required time — not just time for exercise and for cooking more homemade meals, but time to sort through a lot of confusing and sometimes contradictory health information to produce a clear plan of action. Learning new recipes and finding new food ingredients also took surprising amounts of time.

Dean Ornish argues that making major lifestyle changes is in some ways easier and more likely to last than trying to change a little at a time. Certainly that was my experience. Big changes created noticeable results. I lost weight fairly steadily without feeling hungry. By dropping substantially the amount of salt, sugar, and fat in my diet, my taste buds adjusted — things tasted sweet with much less sugar, and rich with much less fat. By making firm new rules in certain areas, I didn't have to waste time and energy in "will I, won't I" dithering.

In that first year, establishing new diet and exercise practices took a lot of time and energy. Since those new patterns have become habits, however, it has required only modest amounts of time and energy to maintain them. And given the payoff of feeling healthier and more energetic, it's been easy to follow the new program.

What health risks do you face at the beginning of the second half of life? Are you overweight? A couch potato? Do you smoke? Do you have a family history of heart disease, stroke, diabetes, or Alzheimer's? Do you have high blood pressure or high cholesterol? In the following sections we'll go through a healthy lifestyle checklist.

Exercise

Exercise has a whole slew of health benefits and is the single most important thing you can do to protect yourself against heart disease. Going from being a couch potato to doing 500 calories worth of exercise per week will cut your risk of heart attack in half. Go all the way to burning 2,000 calories through exercise every week and your risk drops by a factor of six. Exercise helps ward off diabetes, osteoporosis, hypertension. It lowers your "bad" cholesterol and raises your "good" cholesterol.

Exercise promotes healthy weight loss. Muscle tissue burns more calories than fat tissue. Sedentary dieting burns both fat and muscle. Dieting with exercise — or even exercise alone — burns fat and adds muscle so that you not only are stronger, but can also eat more without gaining weight.

Exercise reduces stress, and the damage associated with stress, by metabolizing the stress hormones. It prevents constipation, moderates hunger, improves lung function, improves immune function, reduces spinal difficulties, and reduces some forms of cancer, particularly breast and colon cancer. Moderate exercise even improves sex by increasing circulation.[2]

While exercise at any age is helpful, sooner is better than later. It's far easier to maintain muscle mass than to regain it once it has been lost. It is ever so much easier to keep arteries clear than it is to reopen arteries that have become clogged.

There's good evidence that the older we get, the more important exercise becomes to our health. Yet, amazingly, statistics show that older people are less likely to exercise regularly. Kahn and Rowe found, for instance, that fewer than 20 percent of people seventy-five and older exercised regularly.[3] They report that "when over 40,000 post-menopausal women were studied over a seven-year period, those who did regular exercise were 20% less likely to die than those who were sedentary." Furthermore, "another important finding is that the benefits of exercise even go so far as to negate the adverse affects of other risk factors, such as smoking, high blood pressure and high blood sugar!"[4]

Aerobic exercise — walking, running, cycling, or swimming — has the broadest range of health benefits and is the key to cardiovascular health. That doesn't mean you can neglect training for flexibility and strength later in life — far from it. It is not a requirement of old age to be shrunken and hunched over. Disuse, not aging, is responsible for most such changes. Watch seniors who do regular yoga or Tai Chi and you'll find octogenarians with a greater range of motion than the average forty-year-old. Muscle and connective tissue do become less flexible as we age, which means that it's much easier to retain flexibility than it is to get it back. This loss of flexibility also means that listening respectfully to your body works a lot better than being macho with it. Injuries are one of the prime reasons those over fifty stop exercising.

The idea that an older adult should "pump iron" may be derided by many people, but it can be literally life-changing in its impact, even — and perhaps especially — at a ripe old age. Rowe and Kahn cite one study of a weight-lifting program for seniors in their eighties and nineties. Three times a week for eight weeks they did thirty minutes of weight-lifting on tradi- tional weight machines. Over the course of the eight weeks, par- ticipants' muscle strength increased by 174 percent and walking speed by 50 percent. One weight-lifting session per week was all that was required to maintain these gains.

Strength exercises offer numerous health benefits, but perhaps the most important is improving a person's balance. Falls cause 250,000 hip fractures among older people in the United States every year. Between 10 and 15 percent of such hip fractures are fatal, and many of the remainder result in lasting disability. Strength exercises not only prevent the weakening of bones through osteoporosis, but also make it far less likely that a per- son will fall in the first place.

In lives that are too busy, exercise is often solitary, hurried, and boring. It requires huge amounts of willpower. One of the advan- tages of having time to have a life is that there are more opportu- nities to be physically active in ways that are pleasurable. So rather than approaching exercise like a New Year's resolution, begin exploring how you can link physical activity to other pur- poses. How can you make it a pleasure rather than a chore? The following questions can help you with this process:

✧ **How can I make exercise social?** When I go running with a friend, it always seems to go faster — and I'm less tempted to cut out early — than when I run on my own. Exercise can also be a good way to meet people through hiking clubs or exercise classes.

✧ **How can I make exercise beautiful?** Hiking in natural sur- roundings is much more inviting than walking on a treadmill. Music can make walking or cross-country skiing more pleasant.

✧ **How can I centre myself through exercise?** What forms of exercise are useful for clearing my mind of clutter? What forms of exercise are meditative?

✧ **How can I make exercise fun?** The creative expression of dance makes exercise feel like play rather than work. Sports make exercise both social and playful.

✧ **How can I make exercise multi-purpose?** I use a bicycle for most of my short errands and visits around town. It's better for the environment than driving, and it's cheaper. When I do thirty miles of bicycling a week, I've done three-quarters of my recommended weekly exercise total before I begin "exercising."

✧ **How can I build in regular exercise?** Setting up regular weekly walks, hikes, or runs with friends makes exercise automatic. Weekly classes or sporting activities at the local recreation centre will serve the same purpose.

✧ **How can I get variety?** Varied exercise is more likely to meet our needs for strength, flexibility, and cardiovascular fitness. It also reduces the risk of straining or damaging any particular body part, and it prevents boredom.

I find that when I tie exercise to various other pleasures and purposes, it takes far less willpower. And because I meet my needs for exercise in a variety of ways — bicycling, dance, wallyball, running, walking with friends, and occasional yoga — no one type of exercise feels onerous.

Weight Loss

Weight loss is often the first issue people want to address when they have more time in their life. If you're feeling a little chunky, there are some good reasons to want to slim down in the second half of life: looking trimmer and slimmer, feeling better, the 6+ years that are added to your life expectancy.

Sustained weight loss, however, seems to happen more easily as a secondary goal than as a primary goal. Most people will shed extra pounds slowly but steadily if they seek to get physically fit and shift to a healthier diet. (If you're only willing to do one or the other, exercise has the better track record as a route to sustained weight loss.)

Dieting to lose weight is a high-risk strategy. Ninety percent of dieters gain back within five years whatever weight they lose. Why is that? Most diets cause weight loss by restricting calorie intake. There's enough hunger and deprivation involved that eventually a person runs out of willpower and the pounds go back on. What's worse, any severe restriction on calories will trigger the body into the vigilance stress response described in Chapter Two. The body hunkers down to survive the "famine." It wrings more calories from whatever food you eat, and it burns those calories more efficiently. The vigilance response will also make you reluctant to expend energy, so it sabotages the will to exercise.

The results that come from a health and fitness focus are usually less flashy — you may lose only half a pound to a pound of weight per week — but less willpower is required, and the weight is much more likely to stay off permanently.

Shifting to a Healthier Diet

Are you happy with your current diet? In a too-busy life, nutrition, and sometimes even the enjoyment of food, can be neglected. Prepared and convenience foods can be terribly seductive. It's easy to develop poor eating habits and to wear the consequences of those choices around your middle.

We saw in Chapter Two how a diet based on prepared and convenience foods tends to be deficient in vitamins, minerals, essential oils, and dietary fibre and overloaded with sugar, salt, and fat. It's a diet that has produced epidemics of obesity, heart disease, cancer, diabetes, and hypertension. Nonetheless, it's what most North Americans are used to. It's what we know how to cook. Habit makes it taste good. It's what our friends eat. It's what our kids want to eat. How do you change all that? And where is the freedom in doing so?

For most people, the health risks of a poor diet are too abstract, too quixotic, and too far out in the future to be an effective motivator in the face of all these pulls to stay the same. I found that I felt more impetus to change when I made it an empowerment issue for myself. I was taking charge of food in my life. I was regaining control over what went into my body. Rather than eating fearfully to avoid disease, I sought to eat in ways that made me feel healthy, that gave me more energy, that made it easy to lose the extra pounds I was carrying.

I read books and measured their advice against my own experience. I learned to read labels. I experimented to see what worked best for my body. I felt more freedom around food rather than less.

As soon as you put the words "healthy" and "diet" together, many people assume it is going to mean deprivation and giving up things they crave. If you approach a change in diet that way, you will almost certainly fail. My experience is that few people can stay with a new dietary regimen unless they enjoy it more than their previous eating pattern. So the challenge is to find a new mix of food that tastes as good as or better than what you ate before. Do that and you'll have no trouble keeping to a new diet.

There are several factors that help make a healthier diet a more pleasurable one:

✧ **More taste opportunities.** The volatile organic compounds that refining removes from prepared foods are the tastiest and most aromatic parts. The fibre in whole foods offers texture opportunities not available in refined foods.

✧ **Tastes change.** It usually takes about a month before new foods achieve the comfort of the familiar. Foods that tasted good in the past start to taste too salty, too sweet, and too greasy.

✦ **Hunger-free weight loss.** Fat is extremely calorie-dense. A pound of butter contains as many calories as ten to twenty pounds of green vegetables. When you strip the fat out of food, you strip out a huge number of calories. You can literally eat more food and still lose weight.

✦ **An energy bonus.** The simple carbohydrates in most refined foods tend to create blood sugar crashes and leave you craving snacks. Whole foods tend to deliver a more even flow of energy to the body.

✦ **We are creatures of habit.** Changing your diet can seem like an overwhelmingly large task until you realize that most people select 80 percent of their evening meals from just twelve meal plans. If you can find twelve healthy dinners you enjoy more than what you have now, you've got the core of a new diet.

If you want to develop a new relationship with food, it's helpful to keep a few points in mind:

✦ **You need to make it a focus.** Commit to investing time and energy in food and diet for six months to a year.

✦ **Get support.** When both partners in a couple commit to change, the likelihood you'll make the change is much stronger. It's stronger still if your can convince a couple of your friends to come along for the ride.

✦ **Taste is a prerequisite.** A new food, or a new recipe, may taste better the third or fourth time than it does the first. Aside from that caveat, healthy food also needs to taste good or you'll slide back to the old ways.

✦ **Don't imprison yourself.** Trying to be too perfect in a new dietary regimen can be a pain. I like Dr. Gabe Mirkin's "Rule of Nineteen": If you eat good, healthy food for nineteen of the twenty-one meals in any given week, your body can cope with almost any indiscretion on the remaining two.

Having developed an eating pattern for myself that tastes better, feels better, and has helped me lose weight, I feel some urge to share what has worked for me. I am resisting that urge because I don't believe everyone's food needs are the same, and I think there's real value in the learning process. I will, however, mention four issues most frequently identified as crucial in the nutrition literature.

Whole Foods

One of the things that surprised me when I started reading labels more carefully was how many prepared and convenience foods contained added salt, sugar, *and* fat — all three was the norm. By reading labels and choosing carefully, it is possible to reduce this background intake of salt, sugar, and fat. Making foods yourself, from scratch, gives you even more control over how much salt, sugar, and fat is in your diet. Whole foods also tend to have more vitamins, minerals, food enzymes, and fibre, with fewer chemicals and preservatives.

Fat

There's abundant evidence that the standard North American diet, with 40 to 45 percent of its calories coming from fat, has probably twice as much fat as is optimal.

One of the things that has become obvious to me as I lead heart health classes is that most North Americans *think* they know where the fat is in their diet, but they don't. I've seen people turn down a steak dinner because they're trying to cut down on fat, then scarf down a bag of peanuts without realizing that little snack contained three times as much fat as the dinner did.

Another time I went to a friend's place for a low-fat vegetarian meal. I'm sure my host had absolutely no inkling that her "low fat" walnut-cheese casserole derived more than 60 percent of its calories from fat!

Most prepared and refined foods have added fat. Most snack foods are loaded in fat — often more fat than is contained in a whole meal, including dessert. If you don't read labels, or don't understand what those labels mean, you'll be making blind choices.

Did you know that fish, chicken, turkey, tofu, and wild venison all have about a third the proportion of fat calories that beef, pork, lamb, ham, and cheese do?

A big chunk of the fat in most people's diets is vegetable oil. Different cooking methods — baking, broiling, and sauteeing — can create flavour without fat. Oil-based salad dressings often contain more calories than the salad itself. Tasty alternatives are available. It's misleading to talk of "good fats" and "bad fats." Yes, saturated fats and trans-fats do carry extra health risks. Yes, the body does need a certain intake of essential fatty acids for optimal health. But all fats are calorie-dense foods that make it easy to eat too many calories.

It became clear to me as I began learning where the fat was in my diet that while some fat was flavourful, much of it was invisible precisely because it offered only a tiny flavour dividend. Cutting the least flavourful half of your fat intake requires far less willpower than reductions in the flavourful half, but you have to know where it is to be able to do so.

Veggies

One of the least controversial nutrition ideas is that most North Americans would benefit from eating more fruits and vegetables. Raw veggies in particular are loaded with vitamins, minerals, enzymes, and fibre — and they are low in calories.

However, eating vegetables has become such a joyless, puritan virtue. You're told to eat your plain, cooked-to-mush broccoli because it's good for you. You avoid calories with a salad consisting of limp iceberg lettuce.

The only way you're likely to eat more fruits and veggies is to invest some time and energy in finding ways to make them *tasty*. Cuisines from other parts of the world often do a better job of making vegetables pleasurable. Vegetarian cuisine is also strong in this regard, and the resulting salads can be delicious and incredibly varied. What's required is not grit-your-teeth willpower, but succulent recipes.

The Carbohydrate Hierarchy

In whole foods, sugar and starch are usually bound up with fibre in large chunks. It takes hours for the digestive system to break down these chunks and absorb the food energy of the sugar and starch.

In contrast, when foods are refined, sugar and starch are stripped of fibre and broken into tiny particles, which means they are absorbed far more rapidly — so fast they're practically mainlined into the bloodstream. The body's insulin system goes into overdrive to keep blood sugar levels from skyrocketing. Often the insulin system overshoots, causing a blood sugar crash of low energy.

Simple carbohydrates are a huge strain on the insulin system. The boom-and-bust energy pattern of digesting them makes us crave frequent snacks, so the insulin system never gets a rest. The extra calories in those snacks are usually stored as fat, and an increase in body fat decreases insulin's effectiveness in the body. By mid-life, the insulin system may start to wear out, making many people more sensitive to simple carbs.

Nutritionists often talk of "complex carbohydrates" as if they were a totally different creature from simple carbs, when in fact the complexity of carbohydrates is a hierarchy. Whole grain flours are modestly slower to digest than white flours. Brown rice is modestly more complex than white. Because the particles are larger, stoneground flour is slower to digest than machine-ground flour. Split grains like bulgur and kasha are slower again, whole grains slower still. Undercooked foods release their carbohydrate energy more slowly and evenly than do overcooked foods.

Eating carbohydrates fewer times a day puts less stress on the insulin system. Eating carbohydrates with other foods, especially vegetables, lets them release their energy more slowly.

Once you understand the carbohydrate hierarchy, you can experiment to find an eating pattern that delivers steadier energy and eliminates snack cravings. For many people, changing their carbohydrate eating pattern can be more important to weight loss than reducing fat intake.

Getting Started

There's lots of controversy in the field of nutrition. Almost any dietary prescription you name will have advocates and detractors. There are active debates about vegetarianism vs. meat-eating, organic vs. not. This surfeit of information makes it tempting to throw up our hands and say, "No one really knows. I'll just eat what I want."

I think a more effective strategy is to read a variety of different viewpoints. Look for what reflects your experience with food. Experiment. Use your reading as an aid to discover what works best and what feels best for your body.

Where to start? Dr. Gabe Mirkin brings a great deal of common sense to his books. *Dr. Bob Arnot's Guide to Turning Back the Clock* is a trifle macho for my taste, but if you read selectively you'll find many good ideas on how to use changes in diet and exercise to slow the aging process. If you are suspicious that carbohydrate sensitivity is an issue for you, Richard and Rachael Heller's *Healthy for Life* is probably a good place to start. If you have a history of heart disease in your family, or any evidence of active heart disease, I would recommend *Dr. Dean Ornish's Program for Reversing Heart Disease*. If I had to pick one favourite cookbook, it would be *Fabulous Fat-Free Cooking* by Lynn Fischer.[5]

Bon Appetit.

Smoking and Other Addictions

Young people have enough excess reserve capacity to get away with smoking. Continue that addiction past forty, though, and it is likely that both the quality and the quantity of the second half of your life will suffer.

Did you know that more smokers die from heart disease than from lung cancer? Cancer and heart disease make up about two-thirds of your risk of dying at mid-life. Quit smoking and you slash both risks.

The day I wrote this section, Jim Bacon, the fifty-three-year-old premier of Tasmania, a thirty-five-year smoker, resigned from office after discovering he had inoperable lung cancer. His parting words: "The message from me to everyone is please don't be a fool like me — don't keep smoking."

Willpower alone is often not enough to break free of addictions. If you're serious about breaking an addiction to cigarettes, make a plan for change. Find support for yourself.

If you've been using cigarettes, alcohol, or drugs to try to avoid unpleasant feelings, you may need help dealing with those feelings in order to break free of your addiction.

The Muscle Between Your Ears

What's your worst fear of growing old? Going senile, perhaps, or losing your memory to Alzheimer's disease? Did you know that how you're living now, in your forties and your fifties, has a huge impact on whether you'll keep all your marbles later in life?

When you start to forget things, it's tempting to think of your brain as being like an older car. You want it to last, so you don't drive it as much. That doesn't work. Researchers at Case Western Reserve University found the risk of Alzheimer's disease was three times lower for people who were intellectually active in their forties and fifties than for those who were not.[6] Three times! If your doctor had a pill that could reduce your risk of senility by two-thirds, she'd risk charges of malpractice if she did not recommend you take it.

Rowe and Kahn's results mirror those of other studies on cognition and aging: the general rule is use it or lose. People who found ways to keep using their brains — even activities as simple as crossword puzzles — lost their cognitive abilities much more slowly than those who left their brains in "park." More brains rust out than wear out.

David Snowdon's research had a particular focus on mental functioning in old age. His study participants followed a pattern seen in many studies. Those with more education aged more slowly. Those who continued to challenge themselves with formal or informal learning situations tended to retain mental sharpness much longer than those who did not. Those who were socially well-connected had a reduced risk of developing Alzheimer's, as did those who exercised regularly. Those who were depressed suffered an increased risk of Alzheimer's disease.

Sleep difficulties may become more common as we get older. Poor or inadequate sleep can sabotage the health, energy, and alertness benefits that otherwise come with diet and exercise changes. Often the combination of less stress and more exercise is sufficient to banish insomnia. However, if sleep difficulties persist, learning more about good sleep hygiene can usually solve insomnia problems. Peter Hauri's *No More Sleepless Nights* is a good resource.[7]

Did your mother or father fade into senility at a relatively young age? Have you started forgetting people's names? Don't let fear make you future-phobic. There is a plethora of proven strategies for keeping the brain young. Dr. Gary Small's *The Memory Bible* contains dozens of suggestions on ways to improve "brain fitness" and minimize the environmental agents that speed up the aging process. As Dr. Small, director of the UCLA Centre on Aging, points out, "Memory loss is not an inevitable consequence of aging . . . We can improve our memory performance immediately and stave off, perhaps even prevent, future memory decline."[8]

Healthspan versus Lifespan

In recent years, despite a rapid increase in the number of seniors in North America, the number of disabled seniors and the number of seniors living in care facilities have been relatively stable. Rates of physical and mental disability in the senior population have been dropping almost as quickly as the senior population has gotten larger.

The reason? Health analysts argue that "healthspan" — the number of years a person lives without physical or mental disabilities — has been rising faster than lifespan because of a combination of improved medical care and healthier lifestyle practices. By investing a modest amount of time and energy into developing healthy lifestyle habits early in the second half of life, you can become part of that happy trend. More important than adding years to your life, it will add life to your years.

CHAPTER TEN

Do It Together

Over the past seven chapters we have explored seven facets of freedom in the second half of life: purpose, connection, challenge, money, work, balance, and health.

When I look back at my own process of breaking free, the main thing I would do differently if I knew then what I know now is to seek more support for myself in the difficult and sometimes scary process of change. Related to this, many of the people I would most like to play with are still being ground down by the OverWorld — they have neither the time nor the energy to be good playmates. My freedom would feel richer still if I could share it with more of my friends.

The way I see it, to be free alone is to win the booby prize. If I am the only one free, I will feel lonely, impotent, and irrelevant. There's little point in being free unless we can be free *together*.

Stage One: Create a Support Circle

If you are ready to be wild and free in the second half of life, who do you want to join you on that journey? If you can gather even half a dozen compatriots who will encourage and support you, it will make the whole journey easier and more fun. Your circle doesn't have to meet as an organized group — although that may have value too — but you need people you can feel free to check in with whenever you feel discouraged, confused, or unsure of your path. I can suggest several types of people who would be good to have in your inner circle of support.

Your Spouse

If you have a spouse or significant other, he or she is the first person you'll want to get onside. Perhaps you can sense your partner is ready. Maybe all you need to do is hand over this book when you've finished this chapter.

Or perhaps you need to do some negotiating. Remember that voluntary simplicity is not an either/or thing but a continuum. You need to decide how frugal you want to be. Putting work in its place will slow down the rate at which you can pay off debts and/or save. There's a balance to be struck between freedom now and freedom later. Do you have a shared vision of what you will do when you're free? If you both want freedom but want it in different ways, how can you make the two views of freedom mesh?

If your spouse is locked into a mega-career or consumerism, don't bother challenging that, at least not initially. Start by exploring what the two of you might want to do once you retire. Dreaming together can unite a couple around a shared goal or vision. The breaking-free part then becomes the answer to the question, What's in the way of having what we want?

If your spouse remains uninterested, you need to figure out where that leaves you. How are the two of you going to handle any differences around money? How can you enjoy freedom on your own without being pulled away from your spouse?

More than once I have seen partners who were initially resistant come on board when they see their spouses looking happier and more relaxed.

Friends

If you had more time in your life, who are the people you would most like to play with? If you were going to tackle some thorny social problem in your community, who are the people you'd most want to have with you on the organizing committee?

Who are your best friends? What "carrot" would induce them to break free? How can you encourage them to join your support circle?

Who among your current circle of friends and acquaintances would be supportive of the "Enough Already" idea? Think about all the people you know through community organizations, recreation activities, religious or political organizations. Who do you know who has expressed "Enough Already" urges?

Workmates

Recently I gave an "Enough Already" workshop to the staff of a mid-sized mental health organization. This group of people really enjoyed each other and found the nature of their work stimulating and rewarding. The problem was, there was just too much of it. Staff routinely put in long hours in demanding jobs. They were tired and stressed out. The agency was chronically short-staffed because one or several staff members were always on stress leave. Part-time options were discouraged, and a move was afoot to force existing part-time staff to either work full-time or leave. The staff desperately wanted and needed more balance in their lives. Individually they had few options, and those options involved leaving behind work and workmates they loved. If they were to work together, more might be possible.

Most organizations today want their employees to give their best and to give their all. The lie that organizations tell themselves is that it is possible to have both.

People's "best" can be truly awesome. The creativity and productivity that is possible when people are fresh, when they want to be there, is truly astounding. At least some of the time, employees' "all" includes their best. Unfortunately, if staff are exhausted or cranky, if they don't want to be there, their "all" includes a lot of hours when their productivity is somewhere between mediocre and minimal.

Low-productivity hours are not the worst of it. If people are tired and distracted, they're much more likely to make stupid mistakes or cause accidents. Mistakes and accidents can cost an employer thousands or millions of dollars. When people are cranky they get shirty with the customers, and the customers go somewhere else. When employees are overstressed for too long they burn out, and the employer must spend tens of thousands of dollars on absenteeism and long-term disability costs.

"Speaking truth to power" is a Quaker expression that recognizes the transformative power of a carefully told truth. The truth about overwork is that employers pay just as much for low- or negative-productivity hours as they do for high-productivity time. Buying low- or negative-productivity staff time is a bad bargain for any employer. In that truth your power lies.

Most organizations find it hard to let go of the fantasy that an employee's best and an employee's all are the same thing. They don't want to know about the huge number of low-productivity hours they buy from their employees. They usually need to be dragged reluctantly to the truth, kicking and screaming.

If you raise the issue on your own, you are likely to be scapegoated as a troublemaker. The only time you may be heard is when you and a whole crew of your workmates raise the issue together and keep raising the issue until your employer understands.

Who are your friends at work? Enroll them in the idea of freedom. Not only will they be important allies in the struggle to put work in its place, but they can also be playmates when you have time to play.

Kindred Souls

It's nice to round out your support circle by bringing some new friends into your life.

Juliet Schor reports that 19 percent of Americans voluntarily downshifted between 1990 and 1996. Since then the trend has only grown stronger.[1] The number of people across North America who have embraced voluntary simplicity, who have put work in its place, and who are seeking a new freedom for themselves is now measured in the tens of millions, and the number is growing. Some of those people must live in *your* neighbourhood. How can you find them? You might try the following places:

- ✦ **Volunteer organizations.** Service organizations of all kinds — food banks, Habitat for Humanity affiliates, service clubs — attract those who have already found freedom. Go where your own interest is.
- ✦ **Play groups.** People who have put work in its place will be disproportionately represented in all recreational organizations and activities. When you do whatever you do for fun, be sure to identify yourself as a "person with time."
- ✦ **Voluntary simplicity support groups.** Support groups based on the "Your Money or Your Life" program are springing up all over. You can find them through the New Road Map Foundation.
- ✦ **Show yourself.** Find some way to get yourself profiled in the local media doing whatever has excitement for you. This will make it easier for kindred souls to find you.

Be Good to Yourself

In the early stages of becoming a free being, your focus will be on breaking free of the "over" burden, handling the money issue, putting work in its place, recovering your balance. It's hard work. Your support circle can encourage and support you as you choose a new and different path for yourself. Its members will hold your hand when you get scared, cheer your successes, sympathize with your struggles.

As you increase the amount of time you have available for play, they will be your playmates when the rest of the world is exhausting itself in industrial-strength overwork. They will be your sounding boards and sparring partners as you wrestle with figuring out what you're going to do with the rest of your life. As you get clearer on where you want to go, they will form an inner circle of co-conspirators for whatever experiment, adventure, micro-business, or community-building project seizes your imagination. (Remember that the direct translation of the word "conspire" is *to breathe together*.)

When I was writing this book I asked a dozen friends to help me with ideas and feedback. I called them my "Feedback Circle," but they were a support circle by any other name. Together we have created a book ever so much better than what I could have produced on my own. They also made the process of writing less lonely and kept me going at times when I was ready to say "Enough Already" to the whole project. Next time, I'm not waiting till I'm halfway through the second draft to recruit a support circle. It will be there from the start. Circles have power. Support yourself with the power of the circle.

Stage Two: Expand the Circle

Initially I felt shy and embarrassed about being free of the need to work at age fifty. I tried to be discreet about enjoying my life as a free being.

If you find yourself free of the need to work for money at a young age, you're probably going to have some of the same feelings. It is delicious to feel able to live as a free being in the world. It is not good to feel like you need to hide feeling good. Furthermore, you have a responsibility to your friends and to the planet to communicate the joys that come with freedom.

The freedom that you are enjoying could be equally enjoyable for your friends, workmates, and neighbours. Helping them find their own path to freedom is a gift you can offer them.

There's no need to wait until you've achieved financial independence to encourage others to join you on that path. You may be able to share tools, organize a car co-op, or share the use of a cottage. You could make bulk purchases of food and home supplies together. When you all reach financial independence, you can play together and work together on various projects to build a stronger and more caring community.

Finding Allies

Once you've had a year or two to recover your balance, clean up any bad lifestyle habits, and think about what you want to do next, there's a good chance you'll need to find more allies to do what you really want to do.

In her gentle and thought-provoking book *Turning to One Another,* Meg Wheatley observes that a great many of the most important organizations, events, and activities that happen in communities begin with a group of friends sitting around a kitchen table, talking about what is important to them. When any small group of friends discovers a shared sense of vision or purpose, it can be the nucleus around which larger projects grow.[2]

If there are half a dozen people in your support circle, and each of you enrolls another half dozen people from your community into the breaking free path, that's thirty-six people in your community who are available to be allies in building a stronger sense of community. Whatever your community needs — traffic calming, more daycare, affordable housing, a car co-op, a piece of wilderness protected — there's a core cadre of allies who can work together to make it happen. Thirty-six people with time, energy, and commitment can be a powerful force. Collectively, you'll be able to do a whole lot. If there are enough of you, no one will get overloaded or burned out.

The bigger the job you take on, the more help you need. Sometimes that involves enrolling your friends in the idea of freedom. Other times it means finding the people in your community who have already liberated themselves.

How can you find them? Start with all the places I earlier suggested you look for support circle members: service clubs, recreation associations, community organizations. If you do a search on the Internet, you'll find a number of support organizations for volunteers wanting to create social change, including the following:[3]

✧ Center for a New American Dream (**www.newdream.org**)
✧ Civic Ventures (**www.civicventures.org**)
✧ New Road Map Foundation (**www.newroadmap.org**)
✧ Seva (**www.seva.org**)
✧ Too Young To Retire (**www.2young2retire.com**)
✧ Volunteer Match (**volunteermatch.org**)
✧ International Work Camps (**www.vfp.org**)
✧ Conversation Cafés (**www.conversationcafe.org**)

Don't restrict your search to people of your own age group. There's a huge population of seniors who have refused the enforced idleness of traditional retirement. Feisty seniors with decades of experience being engaged and involved elders, activists, and community leaders can be powerful mentors, models, and inspirations for those of us who are just beginning the journey. As well, a substantial minority among the children of baby boomers have seen what the OverWorld did to their parents and want no part of it. They're natural allies, and they'll think you're "cool."

Learning to Live as a Lightning Rod

In a society where most people feel overworked, overspent, and overstressed, it's easy to feel guilty about being time-rich. It's tempting to keep a low profile to avoid being a lightning rod for other people's envy. I used to tell myself I shouldn't let others know about my good fortune because it would just make them unhappy about what they couldn't have. This feeling was reinforced when I ran into people who acted as though any leisure I had, I must have stolen from them.

When I took a closer look, however, I realized many of the people who were most resentful of my freedom had more financial assets than I did. Any one of them could do what I had done. If they were clearly choosing money as more important to them than time, resentment was a non sequitur. Either they didn't see that they had choices, or they wished they could do what I was doing but, for whatever reason, would not allow themselves to do so.

That's when I decided it was important that I not hide, that I come out as a free being, a manifestation of the choices that are available in the second half of life.

When others poked in sarcastic little "Must be nice" asides after hearing about my next adventure, I began pushing back. "Yes, it is nice," I would say. "Is it something you want to do?" When they told me the various toys and perks they would have to give up in order to live as I did, I would respond, "Oh, so having those things is more important to you than having more time. That's a valid choice, but you should remember it is a choice."

Sometimes when I pushed back I got the "There's so much work to be done in the world, we all need to do our share" argument. This implies that if you're not working for money all the time, you are leaving everyone else to carry your share.

When people took this stance with me, I would agree that it's important we all carry our share of the work that needs to be done. However, I would point out, there's no shortage of people willing to do the paid work in society. In fact, there are millions of North Americans who want paid work but can't find jobs. If anyone should feel guilty it's the people holding down two and three jobs so they can buy expensive toys. They are hoarding a scarce commodity, and other people suffer for their greed.

I would also point out that the main area where there's a shortage of labour is the unpaid economy. There just aren't enough volunteers in North America to do all the unpaid work a caring society needs. By working fewer paid hours, I was making myself available to carry my share of this volunteer load.

Some people will try to convince you that it is practically un-American to not want more. You can make the case that the self-centred pursuit of fame and fortune is a recent cultural value, while thrift, frugality, and helping your neighbour are the pioneer values that built North American civilization.

Other people will argue that buying things creates jobs. If no one spends money, the whole economy will collapse. You can counter that a jobs strategy of permanent growth has made North America dependent on Middle Eastern oil and has devastated the natural environment. Or you can point to the example of Switzerland. Where America has had 3 percent growth per year over the past decade, Switzerland has had a minuscule 0.3 percent growth per year, a virtually stagnant economy. Yet Switzerland has 4 percent unemployment as opposed to America's 6 percent. The Swiss have a positive balance of trade where America has a huge trade deficit. The Swiss are saving; Americans are not. The value of Switzerland's currency has been rising while the American dollar falls. Growth is not the only way to keep unemployment low.

You'll also hear the taxes argument. If you work less, you pay fewer taxes. If we all did that, the government would go broke. My answer is that while I now pay thousands of dollars less in taxes each year than I did when I worked full-time, I've also opened up a job for an unemployed person. That unemployed person has gone from costing the government thousands of dollars per year in welfare and unemployment insurance benefits to paying thousands of dollars in taxes instead. It might be different when and if we reach a full-employment economy, but until that time the net impact on government finances of my working and spending less is positive.

Be patient when you find yourself in the lightning rod role. What's really going on is that people are attracted to the idea of freedom, but it feels scary to do something different from the mainstream. The OverWorld may be crazy and stressful, but it feels "normal." When people spar with you, they may be confronting their own long-held rationalizations for living in a way that they know inside is crazy and unsatisfying.

Stage Three: The Free Beans Insurgency

I have a pet name for people who have broken free in the second half of life. I call us *Free Beans,* a playful twist on "free beings." I see that there's getting to be more and more of us. I believe that if we Free Beans can find ways to work and play together, we could become a powerful force for change in the world.

My proposal is that we call this revolutionary movement the Free Beans Insurgency — "insurgency" in recognition of our potential to subvert the insanity of the OverWorld. Besides, with those initials we can all wear T-shirts that say "FBI agent."

The Free Beans Pledge

Breaking free of the OverWorld on my own gives me one kind of freedom. Breaking free together with a circle of friends and kindred spirits creates a larger and more joyous freedom. So long as the OverWorld remains in place, however, there will always be harsh limits on my freedom. The OverWorld threatens the future of all of us.

How do we break the power of the OverWorld? It's not enough

to break free of the collective insanity on our own. We have a responsibility to encourage others to join us. It is not primarily a matter of persuasion. I believe the challenge is to make our freedom so attractive that others will be drawn to join us.

Breaking the power of the OverWorld will require a big commitment from all of us who have broken free of its grasp. I have created the Free Beans Pledge to set out the commitment we have to make. As far as I'm concerned, you're not really a Free Bean until you've taken the pledge. It goes like this:

I pledge myself to lead a life so happy and fulfilling that it inspires at least a dozen of my friends, workmates, and acquaintances to become Free Beans themselves.

It's not that hard. You just need to be willing to go public about feeling free, happy, and time-rich.

What happens if each of the twelve people you encourage to take the Free Beans Pledge bring in twelve more people? What happens if all those new Free Beans do the same? What would happen if the ripple kept spreading?

In seven links of the chain we would have thirty-five million Free Beans across North America. That's more than a third of the baby boomer generation. Can you imagine how thirty-five million Free Beans would transform North America?

It won't be that simple, of course. Chain letter structures never reach fruition. Too many of the chains die out, and increasing overlap between the chains dilutes the multiplying effect. Still, change does spread like ripples in a pond.

What's more, change builds upon itself like a gathering storm. When only a few are changing, the response is "Those people are weird." When a large and growing circle is involved, curiosity emerges. "What's going on here?" When a whole throng of people is doing something different, suddenly it becomes the bandwagon everyone wants to join.

I think we're getting close to the breakout point. A number of

trend-spotters have named voluntary simplicity and downshifting as the fastest-growing trends of the twenty-first century. A
majority of boomers past fifty are now saying they want part-
time work in preference to full-time. The wave may be starting to
build.

Remember the brave hopes we had in the 1960s and 70s that
our generation would change the world? We boomers have
indeed changed the world, though hardly in the manner we
hoped. If we continue on our current course, the prime legacy
we will leave our grandchildren is a planet irretrievably broken.

Some of our ideals were naive, were wishful thinking. And
some of our ideals were exactly what the world needed, then and
now. Maybe now we are old enough to show both discernment
and character. Maybe now we are old enough, finally, to stand
up for ourselves and say "Enough Already" to the siren song of
addictive consumerism. Together we might still be able to create
a future more like the one we imagined. I'll grant you it's a long
shot, but hey, taking risks is an important skill everyone needs
to learn in the second half of life.

What would happen if the ripple of change were to grow from
the few to the many? Where might it lead?

Hope for the Environment

How would it affect our relationship with the environment if we
had millions of active people out there, modelling that "enough"
is a more trustworthy path to happiness than "more"? If everyone still locked in the OverWorld could look around and see people who were happier, healthier, more relaxed, with interesting
and adventurous lives, living comfortably on much smaller
incomes, wouldn't the OverWorld start to lose its appeal?

One of the best thumbnail indicators of energy and resource
use is money spent. On average, the less money people spend,
the less energy and resources they consume. If, by our happy
example, we can convince enough of our peers to trade money

for free time, then energy use, resource use, and greenhouse gas emissions will all start to drop.

If North Americans were to cut our energy and resource use in half, that would give us roughly the same per capita energy and resource use as we had in the 1950s — hardly a deprived or uncivilized lifestyle. If that change were combined with a comparable increase in energy efficiency, the two together would be enough to halt global warming in its tracks. It's our best shot at saving the planet.

Jobs for the Next Generation

A second powerful subversion would occur if a large chunk of the baby boomers left the paid workforce. (Better still if we left the workforce gradually, so there'd be time to train our replacements.) We could create full employment in North America, even in a shrinking economy. Can you imagine how the North American workplace would change if labour became scarce over the next several years? If workers felt free to say "no" to job speed-up and unpaid overtime? If they were able to demand a healthy balance between work and family?

Years of high unemployment have kept wages stagnant or falling despite large increases in worker productivity. The result is that most working people are able to produce many more goods and services than their paycheques will allow them to buy. So far we have papered over that gap with increasing indebtedness, but there are limits to how much debt any society can support. Low unemployment will give working people the power to bid wages up to more accurately reflect their productivity.

Finally, an Age of Leisure

By modelling the pleasures of lives of balance, and by creating a temporary window of low unemployment, we could give the people left in the workforce both the motivation and the power to demand more leisure for themselves.

Across Europe there are programs that allow older workers to phase into retirement gradually. There are programs that give parents of young children an opportunity to work a shorter workday. In Sweden, the parents of young children are subsidized to work less. There are countries in Europe where the legal minimum for vacation time is five or six weeks per year. We could have the same programs and benefits in North America if more people understood the importance of leisure.

Parents would have the time to be the kind of parents they wish to be: patient, nurturing, and attentive. Couples would have time for each other — not just time to be parents together, but time to be romantic partners.

The Somebody Revolution

In Chapters Three and Seven I wrote about "somebody" challenges — all those things we can see need to be done in the world, but that aren't getting done. How often have you heard your friends and co-workers make "somebody" statements? What would happen if millions of people could be set free to be somebodies in the world? Better yet, what could they accomplish if they were somebodies *together*?

What kind of society could we create? Think about how much richer our communities would be if there were millions more people who had enough time to be good neighbours, good citizens, and good friends. Think about how much music and art and laughter we could create.

One of the most pernicious myths of free-market capitalism is that if a job is important or useful, the free market will pay for it. The truth is that in almost any field or issue you could name, the most important work that could be done is not being done.

When I first put together a heart disease reversal course, some of my friends were envious and asked, "How come you're allowed to teach such a course when you're not medically trained?" The irony is, of course, that the most envious of my friends were those with medical training. They saw lifestyle medicine as exactly where the health care system should be moving, but damned if they could get paid as medical professionals to do what I was doing. That story could be repeated in virtually any field you can name. Across North America the most innovative, groundbreaking work is usually being done by volunteers. If we had millions and millions more people available to do that work, just think of what we could do.

George Bush was elected president with the support of 24 percent of US voters. In the last US congressional elections, 99 percent of incumbents who ran again were re-elected. When the old Soviet Union had election profiles like that, we said it was clear evidence of a non-democratic, totalitarian state. Canada, with the Liberal Party so firmly entrenched that it appears to be the natural governing party, is hardly any better. Reclaiming our democracy will be a full-time job for thousands of somebodies.

Anyone who regularly visits alternative media websites will be shocked at how many crucially important news stories are never mentioned by America's mainstream news media. TV newscasts, in particular, have become entertainment that masquerades as journalism. More and more of the real journalism is being left to volunteers. The channels that disseminate this information are all run by volunteers. There are job openings for thousands more somebodies.

Nowhere is the need for somebodies more urgent than in relation to the environment. We require more than just new technologies if we are to create true energy efficiency. We must wean ourselves from old infrastructures that currently make change somewhere between difficult and impossible. The dead hand of the past stands in the way of the future. The early stages of developing a new infrastructure for a sustainable society will be non-economic. All of that work will have to be done by somebodies because the free market won't pay for it.

It's easy to feel overwhelmed when you think about what needs to be done in the world. The size of the job is not cause for despair; it just means we have to work to make sure the ripple of change keeps expanding. Once there are millions of somebodies ready to share the load, what needs to get done will get done.

Dancing Our Way to Freedom

It takes courage to choose a new path, even when breaking free feels good, even when breaking free makes you part of something larger. I invite you to take the risk and choose this new path. I invite you to join a revolution that I believe is our best hope for the future, not just as individuals, but for our whole generation and those who follow us.

"Enough Already" are the code words that will get you on board. It's not enough just to think the words. It's not enough just to mutter them under your breath when you're tired of feeling tired. You need to stand up for yourself and say "Enough Already!" in the choices you make each and every day.

In my last book I quoted a verse from a song by Al Giordano that again feels appropriate:

> If I can't dance, I don't want to be
> At your revolution, it's no solution
> If I can't sing and shout, you can count me out.
> I'll dance my way to freedom.

I don't know yet whether the Free Beans Insurgency will prove strong enough to save the planet, whether there will be enough of us, soon enough, to turn the world around. What I do know for sure though is, win or lose, we Free Beans are going to have a Damn Good Time doing our best to make that miracle happen.

APPENDIX A

Ancestors' Gathering Visualization

This visualization originated with a line from Robert Louis Stevenson: "The world is so full of a number of things, I'm sure we should all be as happy as kings."

The visualization may initially cause you to feel guilty about not being more appreciative of the abundances in twenty-first-century North American life, but if you let the viewpoint of your ancestors enter your mind from time to time, it can lead you to feel grateful and rich instead. You might want to ask someone to read this visualization to you out loud so you can listen to it with eyes closed.

One evening a massive alien spaceship appears in the sky above your home. It drops slowly and silently till it lands in your backyard. As you look out around your house, you can see that the rest of the world has stopped, as if it has frozen in place.

A panic starts to rise in your throat, but it is pushed aside by an incredible calmness that superimposes itself on your body and mind. The thought *I will not harm you* appears in your mind, accompanied by such sincerity and truthfulness you feel compelled to trust it.

A huge door opens in the side of the spaceship. What looks like a young college student walks down the stairway that emerges from the door.

"This is not my body," the young person says to you. "I have clothed myself in a shape familiar to you to help you relax. In fact, I am of another species and come from a distant star. I have taken on this form because it's the closest Earth equivalent to my position on my home planet.

"I have come here to carry out my research. On my home planet there are time machines that everyone can use to understand their origins. I want to understand how such a time machine might affect a species like yours, which cannot know its ancestors directly. If you take part in my research, you will be given an opportunity to meet a great many of your forebears, some from tens of thousands of years in the past. You will be able to interact with your ancestors and ask each other questions."

The alien tells you that after the experience is over, you will be given a choice: you can forget that anything happened or you can remember the experience as a particularly vivid and powerful dream.

Now you hear a voice in your head, along with the understanding that the alien is speaking directly to your mind. Part of you wants to run in terror, but you gradually become calm as feelings of safety and well-being flood through you from somewhere else.

The alien student informs you that it has used a time machine to search all the bloodlines that lead back from you. It has found all your ancestors, going back hundreds of generations, and brought a representative sampling to a hall inside the spaceship.

You climb the stairway into the spaceship. Inside there is a great hall filled with hundreds of men and women. Many are dressed in strange and exotic clothes — sometimes only animal skins — and you can hear the buzz of dozens of different languages registering surprise at your appearance.

The alien says that your ancestors have all seen a hologram of the inside of your home and watched you going about your daily business there. With a wry smile the alien informs you that your ancestors are all curious to find out what has become of the family line, so they have many questions for you.

You are led up to a dais in the middle of the large hall, surrounded by hundreds of your distant forebears. The area directly in front of you is empty. A spotlight shines in the middle of that empty circle. The thought appears in your mind that this is called the Question Circle.

A dark-skinned young goatherd wearing an animal skin steps up to the Question Circle. You hear a series of guttural sounds full of hard consonants, but with only the barest of delays, inside your ear the question forms: How do you make the sun shine at night?

As you look around, you can tell that all of your ancestors hear and understand his question too. They are looking expectantly to you for an answer. As you explain what lights and electricity are and that you have then in every room, the goatherd falls to his knees, crying, "Praise be to the creator, for from my loins has sprung the greatest of magicians."

Then an adolescent girl in medieval-looking garb steps up to the Question Circle. When she speaks you hear something that sounds almost like French. In your head you hear: "In your big white box I see strange fruits I have only before seen on the plate of the King himself. Am I, a mere peasant girl, the forebear of a royal line of kings and queens?" You start to say that "everyone" has these fruits, which are called "oranges" and "mangos," but as you speak, you hear in your mind that your "everyone" has been translated as "all in my circle." Again everyone in the room gasps. The young girl cries, "Praise be that my line is now of the royal court."

A roly-poly old man who looks like he could be a merchant from Roman times waddles up to the Question Circle. He beams with pride. "Whenever you want musicians you just summon them with your little magic box," he exults. "And not just one group of musicians, I can hear, but many, some from different lands. Do you actually have several groups of musicians outside your chamber just waiting for your command to play? Are you the richest person in all the world?" You try to explain that the musicians are all "recorded" on "CDs," but you can tell that most people in the room are now looking at you as if you were some sort of magician, and many are clearly nervous to be in your presence.

A serious young man who looks like he could possibly be your great-great-grandfather steps into the Circle. He too seems excited and says, this time in words you can hear with your ears as well as in the echo that forms in your head, "That box thing with the moving daguerreotypes and sound, that seems so amazing I am tempted to believe it is sorcery! Can you actually select what story you want to see?" When you answer, "Of course," you see that almost everyone in the room is again looking at you with something between fear and wonder.

A young man in a brightly coloured robe steps up to the microphone. From his mouth come unfamiliar sounds. The translation is hesitant, but in your mind the idea forms that he notices the "clan paintings" on your "hearth shrine" and wants to know how many of your clan have died. You talk about the people in the photos who have died. The young man seems astonished that you have had to bury so few of your clan and gives thanks to the creator not only that you are obviously rich and powerful, but that the creator has given you special blessings. He asks where the rest of your clan is now. When you reply that they all have their own houses, he falls to his knees and regards you with something approaching awe.

An older man, looking like he may have been a shopkeeper in seventeenth-century Britain, steps into the Circle. "I see what looks like an absolutely amazing quantity of glass in the windows of your home," he says excitedly. "Good quality glass, and two layers of it. Are you this rich because of the family business I started?" he asks hopefully. When you reply that you're hardly rich, it is clear the people gathered in the hall do not believe you.

A young Asian woman in a kimono steps up to the Circle. Her words are measured. "It appears that your invisible servants keep the fires of your chambers stoked even when you are not there. Not even the Emperor in my time had such wealth. And the linens on your bed, they are so white. I can see by your skin that there are no fleas or lice in your bedding. By what magic are you able to free yourself of such vermin?" You try to explain central heating and the science of antisepsis, but are meet with such blank stares that you stop and reply only, "Fortune has smiled upon me." This response is met with nodded agreement and various religious gesticulations from all around the room.

You can continue this guided meditation on your own, making up imagined ancestors. Consider the response of distant ancestors to computers, cameras, cars, antibiotics, and electric stoves. Or better yet, when you turn on an electric light, stare through a plate glass window, or turn up the thermostat on a cold winter's morning, reflect on how not even royalty would have enjoyed such comforts five hundred years ago.

APPENDIX B

Suggested Format for

a Work-Option Proposal

A good work-option proposal should include the following:

1. **Introduction.** Outline in a sentence or two the bare bones of who you are and what you propose.
2. **Job description.** Include your job title, status, department, location, supervisor, a brief description of your duties, and a brief description of your responsibilities.
3. **Back-fill coverage/Redefinition of duties.** List the skills or qualifications your replacement will need and suggest how a replacement might be found. If you have someone in mind, it's good to include his or her resume as an appendix. (This section is usually not necessary for flexitime, compressed workweeks, or telecommuting.)
4. **Time schedules.** Describe your proposed schedule in precise detail. What special arrangements will apply for staff meetings, statutory holidays, and vacation time?
5. **Continuity/Communication concerns.** Describe a workable plan for minimizing disruptions to continuity and information flow. In this section you need to list all potential continuity/communication problems that could result and describe what mechanisms will be used to minimize these problems. Among the issues to be considered are staff meetings, staff memos, urgent calls or crisis situations, unfinished

tasks and follow-up, client continuity, and information exchange.

6. **Suggested benefits package.** Flexitime, compressed work-weeks, telecommuting, banked overtime, and short-term leaves do not normally have any effect on benefit packages. For substantial work-time reductions, benefits must be negotiated. Larger organizations may have existing policies. If these arrangements are comfortable for you, list them. In a smaller organization you can make your own suggestions, meeting your needs while keeping added costs for your employer to a minimum. Among the issues you'll have to consider are, in the US, Unemployment Insurance and Social Security contributions, and in Canada, EIC and CPP contributions; vacation and sick leave; statutory holidays; pension or retirement savings plans; medical and/or dental plans; profit-sharing plans; workplace insurance schemes; seniority; and any other employee benefits you receive.

7. **Costs.** Itemize any costs that will result from your new schedule: i.e., added benefit costs, any extra equipment or workspace that is needed, hiring or training costs. Also list any savings that might result. If your proposed back-fill person receives medical and dental coverage through his or her spouse, mention this as an avoided cost. Sometimes replacement staff are junior and therefore get paid less, or a part-time replacement staffer will also be used for peak coverage, which can reduce overtime costs. Part-time staff typically use less sick time. If your organization keeps absenteeism records, you can sometimes estimate the savings likely to result.

8. **Advantages and disadvantages.** Every change in the workplace must be seen as a trade-off. Your challenge is to show that you have redesigned your job in such a way that the advantages are larger than the disadvantages. Among the possible advantages you could cite are reduced absenteeism and turnover, higher productivity, improved morale, better

peak coverage, extended hours coverage, lunch-hour/vacation/holiday coverage, emergency/overtime coverage, extra skills or specialized skills, health and safety benefits, and cost savings.

9. **Local examples.** Your case will be stronger if you can mention other local employers who have had success with the option you are proposing. It may allay your supervisor's fears if he or she is able to talk to the supervisor of someone who's already on a schedule similar to what you propose. Co-workers and professional associations may be able to help you locate such examples. (Talking to someone already working a schedule like the one you want can be useful to you, too!)

10. **A plan for implementation.** When will the new schedule start? What changes need to be made to bring your new schedule on line, and how will they be made? Will there be a trial period? How will that trial be evaluated? What will happen if the trial is discontinued?

A group or union proposal can follow a similar outline. More detailed information on group proposals is available in *Put Work In Its Place*.

Notes

Chapter One

1. Mortality stats are derived from the *United States Life Tables, 1999* of the Centre for Disease Control, prepared by Robert N. Anderson and Peter B. DeTurk. You can find them on the Internet at **www.cdc.gov/ nchs/data/nvsr/nvsr50/nvsr50_06.pdf**.

Out of every 100,000 American women born, 95,384 will still be alive on their fiftieth birthday and 85,179 will still be alive on their sixty-sixth birthday. Percent dying = (95,384 minus 85,179) / 95,384 x 100 = 10.7 percent. Out of every 100,000 American men born, 91,683 will still be alive on their fiftieth birthday and 76,135 will still be alive on their sixty-sixth birthday. Percent dying = (91,683 minus 76,135) / 91,683 x 100 = 16.96 percent.

If (100 minus 16.96) percent of fifty-year-old husbands, and (100 minus 10.7) percent of fifty-year old wives, live till their sixty-sixth birthday, the percentage of couples in which both are still alive on their sixty-fifth birthday is (83.04 x 89.3) = 74.15 percent.

Out of 100,000 US women born, 95,384 are alive on their fiftieth birthday and 86,283 on their sixty-fifth, for a 90.46 percent survival rate. For husbands seven years older, out of every 100,000, 87,134 are still alive on their fifty-seventh birthday and 64,157 are still alive on their seventy-second, for a 73.63 percent survival rate. Odds of both surviving those fifteen years are 73.63 x 90.46 = 66.60 percent.

One caveat is that these figures are based on people who turned sixty-six in 1999. Life expectancy in the US has been rising, so there is a reasonable likelihood that those born after 1933 will have a longer lifespan and lower mortality during the pre-retirement years. And, of course, those who make smart lifestyle choices also run significantly lower risks.

Differences in mortality patterns between Canada and the US are generally minor. (We Canadians live a little longer.)

2. Anita Bryant Quinn and Dori Perrucci, "Retire Early? Think Again," *Newsweek,* July 21, 2003, p. 43.

3. Lewis Hyde, *The Gift: Imagination and the Erotic Life of Property* (New York: Knopf, 1983).

4. David Bond reports that "in 1935, when Franklin D. Roosevelt created social security in the United States, a man of 65 could expect to live an average of three years in retirement." From David E. and Diane Bond, *Future Perfect: Retirement Strategies for Productive People* (Vancouver: Douglas & McIntyre 2002), p. 14.

5. John W. Rowe and Robert L. Kahn, *Successful Aging* (New York: Random House, 1998).

6. David Snowdon, *Aging with Grace: What the Nun Study Teaches Us About Leading Longer, Healthier, and More Meaningful Lives* (New York: Bantam, 2001).

7. George E. Vaillant, *Aging Well: Surprising Guideposts to a Happier Life from the Landmark Harvard Study of Adult Development* (Boston: Little, Brown & Co., 2002).

8. Snowdon, *Aging with Grace,* pp. 116, 203.

9. Martin E.P. Seligman, *Authentic Happiness: Using the New Positive Psychology to Realize Your Potential for Lasting Fulfillment* (New York: Free Press, 2002), p. 40.

10. Vaillant, *Aging Well,* pp. 207 – 209.

11. Rowe and Kahn, Vaillant, and Snowdon all do a good job of itemizing the necessary losses of aging. For a more complete listing of everything that could go wrong as you get older, see John Jerome, *On Turning Sixty-Five: Notes from the Field* (New York: Random House, 2000).

12. For a more detailed discussion of science's changing attitude to aging see Betty Friedan, *The Fountain of Age* (New York: Simon and Schuster, 1993), Chapters Two and Three.

13. Ibid., pp. 100 – 102.

14. Becca R. Levy et al., "Longevity Increased by Positive Self-perceptions of Aging," *Journal of Personality and Social Psychology,* August 2002.

Chapter Two

1. Juliet B. Schor, *The Overworked American: The Unexpected Decline of Leisure* (New York: Harper-Collins, 1991), p. 2.

2. Cited in *The Jobs Letter* #195, October 29, 2003.

3. Joe Robinson, "Ah, Free at La . . . Oops! Time's Up," *Washington Post*, July 27, 2003, p. B01.

4. Bruce O'Hara, *Working Harder Isn't Working: How We Can Save the Environment, the Economy and Our Sanity By Working Less and Enjoying Life More* (Vancouver: New Star Books, 1993), Chapter Three.

5. Bill Branigin, "US Consumer Debt Grows at Alarming Rate," *Washington Post*, January 12, 2004. The per household figures are derived using US Census estimates of 107.5 million households.

6. Juliet Schor, *The Overspent American: Upscaling, Downshifting and the New Consumer* (New York: Basic Books, 1998).

7. John de Graaf, David Wann, and Thomas Naylor, *Affluenza: The All-Consuming Epidemic* (San Francisco: Berrett-Koehler, 2001), p. 2.

8. Ibid., pp. 4, 14, 19, 64, 85.

9. A good summary of the extremely weak correlation between money and happiness can also be found in Tim Kasser's *The High Price of Materialism* (Cambridge: MIT Press, 2002), p. 3.

10. Chris Sharpley, Renaty Gordon, and Nicky Jacobs, "Results of a survey of adjustment to retirement," release from Monash University, Centre for Stress Management and Research, 1996.

11. Further evidence of this treadmill is the Merck poll finding that the amount of income Americans consider necessary to live in "reasonable comfort" has been rising in tandem with the median income. See Schor, *The Overspent American*, pp. 98 – 99.

12. Schor, *The Overworked American*, p. 115.

13. Schor, *The Overspent American*, pp. 3 – 13.

14. Ibid., pp. 13, 80.

15. For a classic analysis of what does and doesn't create satisfaction in our consumer society see Part One of Paul L. Wachtel, *The Poverty of Affluence* (New York: Free Press, 1983). A more recent examination of the same issues is in Paul L. Wachtel, "Full Pockets, Empty Lives: A Psychoanalytic Exploration of the Contemporary Culture of Greed," *American Journal of Psychoanalysis*, June 2003.

16. See Schor, *The Overworked American*, p. 11, and Stanley Cohen, *Sleep Thieves: An Eye-opening Exploration into the Science and Mysteries of Sleep* (New York: Free Press, 1996), pp. 249 – 256.

17. Najib T. Ayas et al., "A Prospective Study of Sleep Duration and Coronary Heart Disease in Women," *Archives of Internal Medicine* January 27, 2003.

18. Anna Peeters et al., "Obesity in Adulthood and Its Consequences for Life Expectancy," *Annals of Internal Medicine* January 7, 2003. A fifteen-year Finnish study found that obesity also leads to chronic ill-

health: more workplace disability, more coronary problems, and more long-term medication use. See Tommy L.S. Visscher et al., "Obesity and Unhealthy Life-Years in Adult Finns," *Archives of Internal Medicine* July 12, 2004.

Chapter Three

1. Sam Keen, *Hymns to an Unknown God: Awakening the Spirit in Everyday Life* (New York: Bantam, 1994), pp. 227 – 228.
2. George Vaillant, *Aging Well: Surprising Guideposts to a Happier Life from the Landmark Harvard Study of Adult Development* (Boston: Little, Brown & Co., 2002), pp. 45 – 47.
3. Abigail Trafford, *My Time: Making the Most of the Rest of Your Life* (New York: Basic Books, 2004), pp. 23 – 27.
4. Jacqueline Blix and David Heitmiller, *Getting a Life: Real Lives Transformed by* YOUR MONEY OR YOUR LIFE (New York: Viking, 1997).
5. Mihaly Csikszentmihali, *Flow: The Psychology of Optimal Experience* (New York: Harper & Row, 1990).
6. "It Ain't Half Hot, Mum," *Sydney Morning Herald,* August 8, 2003.
7. "Warning of Global Anarchy," *Sydney Morning Herald,* February 24, 2004.
8. The George Bernard Shaw quote was originally in the dedicatory epistle to Shaw's 1903 play *Man and Superman* and is quoted in Bob Buford, *Half Time: Changing Your Game Plan from Success to Significance* (Grand Rapids: Zondervan Publishing, 1994), p. 32.
9. Jacob Needleman, *Time and the Soul* (New York: Doubleday, 1998).
10. Richard J. Leider and David A. Shapiro, *Repacking Your Bags: Lighten Your Load for the Rest of Your Life* (San Francisco: Berrett-Koehler, 1995), and Bob Buford, *Game Plan: Winning Strategies for the Second Half of Your Life* (Grand Rapids: Zondervan Publishing, 1999).
11. Vaillant, *Aging Well*, p. 113.

Chapter Four

1. Dean Ornish, *Love and Survival: The Scientific Basis for the Healing Power of Love and Intimacy* (New York: HarperCollins, 1998), pp. 42 – 45.
2. Tim Kasser, *The High Price of Materialism* (Cambridge: MIT Press, 2002), p. 47.
3. Gail Sheehy, *Understanding Men's Passages: Discovering the New Map of Men's Lives* (Toronto: Random House, 1996).
4. Betty Friedan, *The Fountain of Age* (New York: Simon and Schuster, 1993), pp. 293 – 296.
5. Carolyn Shaffer and Kristin Anundsen, *Creating Community Any-*

where: Finding Support and Connection in a Fragmented World (New York: Tarcher, 1993).

6. John W. Rowe and Robert L. Kahn, *Successful Aging* (New York: Random House, 1998), p. 218.

7. David Snowdon, *Aging with Grace: What the Nun Study Teaches Us About Leading Longer, Healthier, and More Meaningful Lives* (New York: Bantam, 2001), p. 184.

8. George Vaillant, *Aging Well: Surprising Guideposts to a Happier Life from the Landmark Harvard Study of Adult Development* (Boston: Little, Brown & Co., 2002), pp. 70 – 73. "Susan Wellcome" is a pseudonym.

Chapter Five

1. Jane Juska, *A Round-Heeled Woman: My Late-Life Adventures in Sex and Romance* (New York: Villard Books, 2003).

2. Sam Keen, *Learning to Fly: Trapeze — Reflections on Fear, Trust, and the Joy of Letting Go* (New York: Broadway Books, 1999).

3. James Hillman, *The Force of Character and the Lasting Life* (New York: Random House, 1999).

4. Ram Dass, *Still Here: Embracing Aging, Changing and Dying* (New York: Penguin, 2000), p. 24.

5. Ibid., p. 23.

6. George Vaillant, *Aging Well: Surprising Guideposts to a Happier Life from the Landmark Harvard Study of Adult Development* (Boston: Little, Brown & Co., 2002), p. 206.

7. Abigail Trafford, *My Time: Making the Most of the Rest of Your Life* (New York: Basic Books, 2004).

Chapter Six

1. Joe Dominguez and Vicki Robin, *Your Money or Your Life: Transforming Your Relationship with Money and Achieving Financial Independence* (New York: Penguin, 1992).

2. Joe Dominguez, *Transforming Your Relationship With Money,* audiotape workshop (Boulder, CO: Sounds True, Inc, 2001).

3. David K. Foot and Daniel Stoffman, *Boom, Bust and Echo: How to Profit from the Coming Demographic Shift* (Toronto: Macfarlane, Walter and Ross, 1996).

4. Tim Kasser, *The High Price of Materialism* (Cambridge: MIT Press, 2002).

5. Juliet Schor, *The Overspent American: Upscaling, Downshifting and the New Consumer* (New York: Basic Books, 1998), pp. 80-81.

6. John de Graaf, David Wann, and Thomas Naylor, *Affluenza: The All-Consuming Epidemic* (San Francisco: Berrett-Koehler, 2001); Alan Durning, *How Much Is Enough? The Consumer Society and the Future of the Earth* (New York: W.W. Norton and Company, 1992).

Chapter Seven

1. Bob Buford, *Half Time: Changing Your Game Plan from Success to Significance* (Grand Rapids: Zondervan Publishing, 1994).

2. Bruce O'Hara, *Put Work in Its Place: How to Redesign Your Job to Fit Your Life*. (Vancouver: New Star Books, 1994).

3. Barney Olmsted and Suzanne Smith, *The Job Sharing Handbook* (San Francisco: New Ways to Work, 1994).

4. Marsha Sinetar, *Do What You Love, the Money Will Follow: Discovering Your Right Livelihood* (New York: Dell, 1989).

Chapter Eight

1. Theresa L. Crenshaw, *The Alchemy of Love and Lust: Discovering Our Sex Hormones and How They Determine Who We Love, When We Love and How Often We Love* (New York: Putnam, 1996), p. 34.

2. Ibid., p. 47.

3. Ibid., p. 51.

4. Jimmy Carter, *The Virtues of Aging* (New York: Ballantine Books, 1998), p. 79.

5. Julie Morgenstern, *Organizing from the Inside Out: The Foolproof System of Organizing Your Home, Your Office and Your Life* (New York: Henry Holt, 1998).

Chapter Nine

1. John W. Rowe and Robert L. Kahn, *Successful Aging* (New York: Random House, 1998), p. 94.

2. For a comprehensive overview of the health benefits of exercise, see Chapters One and Two of Brian J. Sharkey, *Fitness and Health* (Champaign, IL: Human Kinetics, 2002). For particular health benefits for seniors see Rowe and Kahn's *Successful Aging,* pp. 97 – 110.

3. Rowe and Kahn, *Successful Aging,* p. 142.

4. Ibid., pp. 136 – 137.

5. Gabe Mirkin, *Fat Free and Flavorful: Dr. Gabe Mirkin's Guide to Losing Weight and Living Longer* (Boston: Little Brown, 1995); Robert Arnot, *Dr Bob Arnot's Guide to Turning Back the Clock* (Boston: Little Brown, 1995); Richard F. Heller and Rachael F. Heller, *Healthy for Life:*

The Scientific Breakthrough Program for Looking, Feeling and Staying Healthy Without Deprivation (New York: Dutton, 1995); Dean Ornish, *Dr. Dean Ornish's Program for Reversing Heart Disease* (New York: Random House, 1990); Lynn Fischer, *Fabulous Fat-Free Cooking: More than 225 Dishes — All Delicious, All Nutritious, All with Less Than 1 Gram of Fat!* (Boston: Rodale, 1997).

6. Gary Small, *The Memory Bible: An Innovative Strategy for Keeping Your Brain Young* (New York: Hyperion, 2002), p. 85.

7. Peter Hauri, *No More Sleepless Nights* (New York: Wiley, 1990).

8. Small, *The Memory Bible,* p. vii.

Chapter Ten

1. Juliet Schor, *The Overspent American: Upscaling, Downshifting and the New Consumer* (New York: Basic Books, 1998), p. 113.

2. Margaret J. Wheatley, *Turning to One Another: Simple Conversations to Restore Hope to the Future* (San Francisco: Berrett-Koehler, 2002).

3. For a more complete listing of volunteer support agencies see the Resource List in Marc Freedman's *Prime Time: How Baby Boomers Will Revolutionize Retirement and Transform America* (New York: Public Affairs, 1999). A good Canada-focused Internet resources list can be found in David E. and Diane Bond's *Future Perfect: Retirement Strategies for Productive People* (Vancouver: Douglas and McIntyre, 2002).

Index